T3-BOU-363
THE LIBRARY
ST. MARY'S COLLEGE OF MARYLAND
ST. MARY'S CITY, MARYLAND 20686

Women in Politics and Decision-Making in the Late Twentieth Century

A United Nations Study

United Nations Office at Vienna
Centre for Social Development and Humanitarian Affairs

Women in Politics and Decision-Making in the Late Twentieth Century

A United Nations Study

MARTINUS NIJHOFF PUBLISHERS
DORDRECHT / BOSTON / LONDON

NOTES

In this publication, country names and designations are those that were in use when the data were being compiled.

The designations employed and the presentation of the material in this publication do not imply the expression of any opinion whatsoever on the part of the Secretariat of the United Nations concerning the legal status of any country, territory, city or area or of its authorities, or concerning the delimination of its frontiers of boundaries.

Library of Congress Cataloging-in-Publication Data

Women in politics and decision-making in the late twentieth century : a United Nations study / United Nations Office at Vienna, Centre for Social Development and Humanitarian Affairs.
p. cm.
ISBN 0-7923-1648-7 (alk. paper)
1. Women in public life. 2. Women in politics. 3. Women government executives. I. Centre for Social Development and Humanitarian Affairs (United Nations)
HQ1390.W64 1992
320'.082--dc20 92-2732

ISBN 0-7923-1648-7

Published by Martinus Nijhoff Publishers,
P.O. Box 163, 3300 AD Dordrecht, The Netherlands.

Sold and distributed in the U.S.A. and Canada
by Kluwer Academic Publishers,
101 Philip Drive, Norwell, MA 02061, U.S.A.

In all other countries, sold and distributed
by Kluwer Academic Publishers Group,
P.O. Box 322, 3300 AH Dordrecht, The Netherlands.

Printed on acid-free paper

All Rights Reserved
© 1992 UNITED NATIONS
Kluwer Academic Publishers incorporates the publishing programmes of Martinus Nijhoff Publishers.

No part of the material protected by this copyright notice may be reproduced or utilized in any form or by any means, electronic or mechanical, including photocopying, recording, or by any information storage and retrieval system, without written permission from the copyright owner.

Printed in the Netherlands

PREFACE

The Convention on the Elimination of All Forms of Discrimination against Women[1] and the Nairobi Forward-looking Strategies for the Advancement of Women to the Year 2000[2] reflect the significance that the United Nations attaches to the importance of equality as part of the process of the advancement of women.

In 1990, the Commission on the Status of Women considered equality in political participation and decision-making as a priority theme. The Division for the Advancement of Women of the Centre for Social Development and Humanitarian Affairs of the United Nations Office at Vienna was requested to convene an expert group meeting on the topic as part of the preparations for the thirty-fifth session of the Commission. This meeting was held at Vienna in September 1991. It was attended by 16 experts from all regions. The meeting was chaired by Margaret Alva (India), at the time, Minister of Youth Affairs and Sports, Women and Child Development. Vice-Chairpersons were Gertude I. Mongella (United Republic of Tanzania), at the time, Minister without Portfolio, and Senator Santaninna Rasul (Philippines). Eleni Stamiris (Greece), at the time, Director of the Mediterranean Women's Studies Centre (KEGME), was the Rapporteur.

The meeting brought scholars and political practitioners together to examine the obstacles to women's participation in decision-making and to suggest remedies. It provided an opportunity for the Division for the Advancement of Women to prepare a database on women's participation in governmental decision-making. Two consultants, Kathleen Staudt of the University of Texas in the United States of America and Denise Conroy of the Queensland University of Technology in Australia, prepared and presented studies. Each expert presented a case-study on developments in their country.

The results of the meeting were presented to the Commission on the Status of Women in a report by the Secretary-General entitled 'Equality: Equality in political participation' (E/CN.6/1990/2), and were reflected in resolution 1990/4 of the Economic and Social Council.

Responding to a concern that the information presented to the meeting and the conclusions arising from it should be available to a wider audience, the Government of the Netherlands provided funds to enable the Division for the Advancement of Women to prepare this book, which is based on that material. Monique Leijenaar of the University of Nijmegen in the Netherlands, who was one of the experts at the meeting prepared a first draft of the analysis and, together with Kees Niemöller of the University of Amsterdam, prepared most of the tables and figures shown in the text. The final text was prepared by the Division for the Advancement of Women.

---

[1] Adopted by the General Assembly in its resolution 34/180, annex.

[2] Report of the World Conference to Review and Appraise the Achievements of the United Nations Decade for Women: Equality, Development and Peace, Nairobi, Kenya, 15-26 July 1985 (United Nations publication, Sales No. E.85.IV.10), chap. I, sect. A.

CONTENTS

ANNEXES

TABLES

FIGURES

INTRODUCTION

Few women occupy positions in public decision-making. While their numbers have been increasing slowly in many countries, in most there has been little qualitative change in the situation. Only in a few countries has the proportion of women reached a point where it can be said that their influence on public policy is comparable with that of men.

The minimal participation of women in political decision-making is readily apparent: citizens of most countries can observe it directly whenever government officials appear in the press. What is not known is the precise incidence of women in the decision-making process, and the factors that allow, or impede, their access to top-level public life. While some non-governmental organizations do attempt to monitor the incidence of women in decision-making, there has been no comparative analysis of the situation, particularly in terms of the ratio of men to women in relevant positions. This situation is paradoxical. In 1987, there was only one country where men could vote but women could not. Women have had the franchise, on average, for over 40 years and they often vote in the same proportion as men. Most countries have accepted international legal norms advocating the participation of women in decision-making. Despite this, they are not elected or appointed leaders. Nowhere in the situation of women is the gap between de jure and de facto equality so wide.

It might be argued that participation in decision-making will be facilitated by women's advancement in other areas, including education and formal economic activity. Yet, without their political participation, progress in the other areas may be slow since it is often dependent on resources that come from public sources. There is a close reciprocal relationship between the general advancement of women and the participation of women in decision-making. Women's political participation will be enhanced if social and economic support structures exist, legal discrimination is eliminated and negative stereotypes are banished from education and the media. Increased participation by women in politics may be necessary for improved social, economic, legal and cultural conditions for women. As was stated in Economic and Social Council resolution 1990/15, annex, paragraph 6:

That women are grossly underrepresented in political decision-making has been amply documented. This means that decisions on public policies that affect women's equality are still in the hands of men, who may not have the same incentive to pursue them as women. Despite indications that in some countries women, by voting for candidates or parties that promise to promote their interests, are beginning to decide the outcome of elections, the incidence of , political parties and in formal government is still low. The situation will persist unless more women stand and are selected for office and are allowed to begin careers leading to senior management positions in the public sector and until women exercise their voting power in their own interests as well as in the interests of society.

There are five basic arguments for women's participation in decision-making that have been advanced whenever women have demanded citizenship and, subsequently, an extension of rights. They are also valid arguments in support of their claim to increased representation in politically important posts.

The first argument concerns democracy and egalitarianism. Women constitute at least half of any population and should be represented proportionally. The recognition of women's rights to full citizenship must be reflected in their effective participation at the various levels of political life. There cannot be true democracy where women are virtually excluded from positions of power.

The second argument is one of legitimacy. Women's underrepresentation can be dangerous for the legitimacy of the democratic system since it distances elected representatives from their electorate and more particularly from the women among their electors. The legitimate value of the outcome of political decision-making is thus not the same for both men and women. This may give rise to public mistrust towards the representative system. The final consequence may be that women - in imitation of the Declaration of Sentiments made at Seneca Falls in 1848, in which women declared that the American Constitution was not valid since they had no say in its formulation - refuse to accept laws and policies that have been drafted without their participation.

The third argument is of differences in interests. Political participation involves articulating, providing and defending interests. Women are conditioned to have different social roles, functions and values. It is reasonable to believe that women are more aware of their own needs and are therefore better able to press for them. Women are more aware, for example, of the need to have control over their own bodies and therefore access to family planning; to have proper provision for the care of children and of others who are physically dependent; and to have more protection against sexual violence and harassment. The current composition of the political decision makers means that women are unable to articulate and defend their own interests.

The fourth argument is that of changing politics. There are some indications that women politicians, if there are enough of them, can change the focus of politics. Women are more critical of the traditional definition of politics. An initial effect of women entering the political scene was the enlargement of the scope of politics. Issues, such as child care, sexuality and family planning, that were once confined to the private sphere are now seen as political. Some women have come to regard the decision-making process itself as being too centralized, too hierarchical and too technocratic.

The final argument is for the efficient use of human resources. No country can afford not to utilize all its human resources. Women comprise half the world's pool of potential talent and ability. The importance of their fundamental biological and social roles is clear, and, though their input is often unrecognized, they are major contributors to national economies through their paid and unpaid labour. Excluding women from positions of power and from elected bodies impoverishes public life and inhibits the development of a just society. In short, without the full participation of women in decision-making, the political process will be less effective than it can and should be, to the detriment of society as a whole.

In spite of these arguments, often women are not available for selection or election to public office. The reasons can be extrapolated from an examination of the careers of those women who have become decision makers, and deduced by comparing conditions, such as background factors and institutional arrangements, in countries that have a larger percentage of women in decision-making than many other countries. Several issues are involved. Whether economic development or wealth is a prerequisite for women to become decision makers. Whether different types of party or electoral system help or hinder participation. Whether and to what extent women need the same skills as men to enter politics, and how they get them.

These are not new issues. The organized struggle for political rights, of which the right to vote was one of the first manifestations, began in the middle of the nineteenth century. That issue was not resolved for most women, until the second half of the twentieth century. In 1945, when the Charter of the United Nations was signed, affirming 'faith in fundamental human rights, in the dignity and worth of the human person, in the equal rights of men and women and of nations large and small', less than half the signatory Governments allowed women the unrestricted right to vote. In 1946, the General Assembly, in its resolution 5b (I), recommended 'that all Member States, which have not already done so, adopt measures necessary to fulfil the purposes and aims of the Charter ... by granting to women the same political rights as to men'.

The Commission on the Status of Women, the United Nations intergovernmental body that deals with the advancement of women, adopted the first of many resolutions on women's political participation in 1947, at its first session. It continued that concern over the next 40 years. In 1987, as part of its effort to implement the Nairobi Forward-looking Strategies, the Commission decided to consider the subject of equality in political participation and decision-making in 1990.

To prepare for the Commission's discussion, the Division for the Advancement of Women organized an Expert Group Meeting on Equality in Political Participation and Decision-making at Vienna from 18 to 22 September 1989. This Meeting brought together scholars and parliamentarians from 16 countries. It involved the preparation of background papers and national case-studies, which provided an opportunity to explore the changes that had occurred in women's participation in national decision-making and to examine the types of obstacle women faced in reaching decision-making positions.

The present publication is based on the information prepared for the Expert Group Meeting. Unless otherwise indicated, all the country information in the present book is drawn from the case-studies and working papers prepared for the Meeting. However, where developments since 1989, for example in Eastern Europe, have substantially changed the findings, more recent information has been provided, as noted in the text.

Some of the information is derived from new series developed by the United Nations Statistical Office as a result of the United Nations Decade for Women: Equality, Development and Peace (1976-1985) and included in the United Nations Microcomputer Database on Women's Indicators and Statistics (WISTAT), and data on the incidence of women in national decision-making developed specifically for the Expert Group Meeting. In analysing the various statistics, it has been found that doing so by geographical region summarizes major historical and environmental factors and constitutes a sound basis for combining country data. Data are used from five regions: Africa, Asia and the Pacific, Eastern Europe, Latin America and the Caribbean, and the Western industrialized countries (including countries of Western Europe plus Australia, Canada, New Zealand and the United States).

The focus is on women's participation in formal decision-making at the national level. It does not include activities that are often said to provide alternative channels for women's political participation, local government and informal lobbying or access to those who are in power.

It is often assumed that although they may be underrepresented at the national level, women participate more actively closer to home, at the local level. Some countries report this to be the case, however, there are few figures available for comparison. However, for those countries where data were available in 1989, it was concluded in a report of the Secretary-General entitled 'Peace: Full participation of women in the construction of their countries and in the creation of just social and political systems' (E/CN.6/1989/7) that:

> The participation of women in voting in local elections is comparable to their participation in voting in parliamentary elections. Available sources of information indicate that, in general, the participation of women in local representative bodies is slightly higher than in national parliaments, although the pattern is by no means uniform' (paragraph 55).

In most countries, whatever the impression, in practice, participation in local decision-making is not taken as an alternative to national participation. It is also often assumed that although women do not hold power directly, they exert their influence indirectly and this, in some way, compensates for their absence from governmental positions. There are indeed many examples of women who have strongly influenced state policies through informal channels, for example through their spouses or friends in powerful positions. The French political salons of the nineteenth century are well known. Examples can also be found of women who have been said to have exercised the 'power behind the throne' as the wives of presidents or prime ministers. Jehan Sadat of Egypt, a vocal advocate of women's rights, was the driving force behind the establishment of extra seats in parliament for women during her husband's tenure[3]. In Nigeria, Babangida, the wife of the military president, has been credited with raising and legitimizing questions of gender equality as matters of public concern.[4] The wives of many Mexican officials, from the President down, have taken a leading part in the activities and fund-raising activities associated with the Desarollo Integral de la Familia.[5] As noted in the case-study on Greece, Margarita Papandreou, when wife of the Prime Minister of Greece, used her influence to get women high political posts or nominated as party candidates for elections. But proximity to power is not the same as having it.

---

[3] Nina Mba and Simi Afonja, 'Toward the creation of a new order for Nigerian women: Recent trends in politics and policies', 'Beyond Nairobi: Women's politics and policies in Africa revisited', Kathleen Staudt and Harvey Stickman, eds., special issue of issue: A Journal of Opinion , vol. XVII, No. 2 (1989), p. 7.

[4] Victoria Rodriguez, 'The politics of decentralization in Mexico', doctoral dissertation for the University of California, 1987.

[5] Participation of Women in Decision-making for Peace: Case-study on Greece (United Nations publication, Sales No. E.91.IV.6)

CHAPTER I
PARTICIPATION AS A LEGAL RIGHT

In 1989 there were almost no countries where men could vote or stand for office but women could not. Thus very few women were restricted by legal prohibition, however, a wide gap remains between their de jure right to participate and their actual participation. In Kuwait, for example, women's right to vote is restricted, but elections have been suspended, thus the existing sex differences in the law are without effect. In Switzerland, women's right to vote was still restricted in one half-canton, Lower Alpenzell, in 1989, but the restriction was declared unconstitutional in 1990. So few women are restricted by legal prohibitions.

THE RIGHT TO VOTE

Women's access to formal political power began with the advent of universal suffrage. In some countries the right of women to vote was granted only after prolonged struggles, led by women, the suffragists, began in the mid-nineteenth century. In those countries, mostly in Europe and North America, but also in New Zealand and Australia, opposition to the enfranchisement of women was mainly based on the assumption that women and politics did not belong together. Arguments used to deny women the vote included:

- Women were too emotional and therefore not capable of evaluating political matters;

- Women were already represented through their husbands;

- Women would lose their femininity by interfering with such a 'dirty' matter as politics.

Strategies used by the suffragists included demonstrations, sit-ins, parades, hunger strikes and marches on the parliament. In countries such as the Netherlands, the

United Kingdom of Great Britain and Northern Ireland, the United States, as well as the Scandinavian countries, these activities reached their peak during the period from 1900 to 1920. In some other countries, however, women were still striking and demonstrating for their rights as late as the 1940s and 1950s. In Costa Rica in 1949, women revolted against the laws and ideas that limited women's participation to matters related to marriage, house-work and the care of children. Previously, few women had dared to contradict the established behavioural norms. But in that year, 7,000 women marched in public demanding political rights equal to men.

The right to vote was not always the result of activities of militant women, however. In some countries it followed major long-term changes in the general educational, economic and employment status of women. To the extent that political rights were de facto restricted by economic or educational requirements, the increase in the educational and economic level of women automatically implied the right to vote and stand for election.

Sometimes, the right to vote was bestowed as a reward for women's participation in independence struggles and their contribution to national survival in times of crisis. For example, in India, because they had been particularly active in the independence struggle, equal rights for women were accepted without apparent hostility or resistance as part of the ethic of change accompanying independence. The same was true of some countries in Europe where women acquired the vote after the end of the Second World War, during which they had taken over responsibility for farming and other production and thus broken down the traditional sexual divisions of labour. Nor could Governments ignore their activities in resistance movements, therefore women were granted the vote with little opposition.

The processes by which women obtained the vote are shown in figure I.

Figure I. Dates on which women first received the right to vote

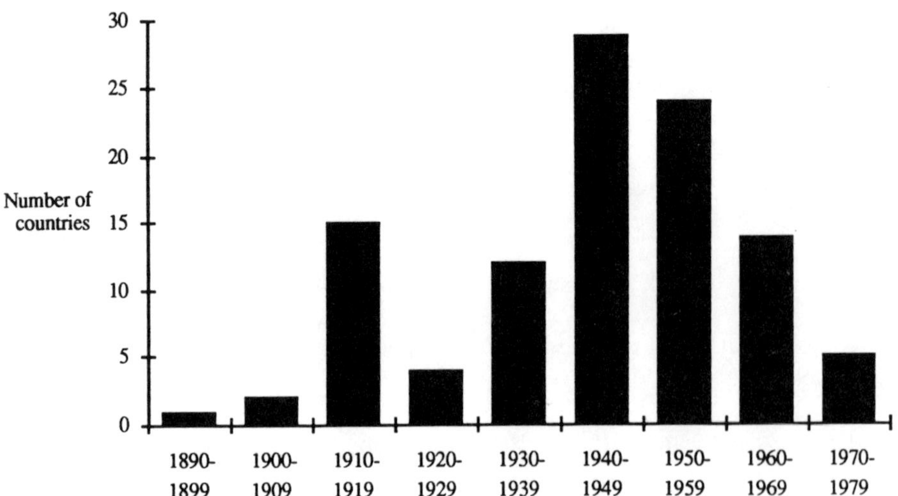

The first country where women obtained the vote nationally was New Zealand (1893), followed by Australia in 1901. Fourteen other countries including Austria, Canada, Czechoslovakia, Denmark, Finland, Germany, Iceland, Ireland, Luxembourg, Netherlands, Norway, Poland, the Union of Soviet Socialist Republics and the United States had granted an unrestricted franchise by 1920. In that period many countries made considerable political changes which eased the way for constitutional provisions allowing women to vote.

A further 16 countries had granted women the right to vote prior to the outbreak of the Second World War. They included Sweden, United Kingdom, Portugal, Spain and Turkey and also many non-European countries, some of which were not then independent. These included Brazil, Burma,[6] Cuba, Ecuador, Maldives, Mongolia, Philippines, South Africa,[7] Sri Lanka, Thailand and Uruguay. Most other countries granted women and men the right to vote in the preparations for independence.

In 1987, women had the right to vote in all of the 115 countries on which the Inter-Parliamentary Union had information. (The Inter-Parliamentary Union is a non-governmental organization, made up of national parliaments, which maintains statistics, including those on women in politics). In some countries, including Bahrain, Bhutan, BruneiDarussalam, Oman, Qatar, Saudi Arabia and the United Arab Emirates, neither men nor women had the right to vote. In these countries, the executive was absolute, there was no democratically elected legislature and, therefore, no periodic elections.

So, by 1987 most women had had the right to vote for all of their adult lives. Data show that women have had on average the right to vote for 39 years, ranging from 97 years in New Zealand to 8 years in Equatorial Guinea, Jordan and Sao Tome and Principe. On a regional basis, the average was 56 years in both Western industrialized and Eastern European countries, 38 years in Asia and the Pacific and in Africa, and 37 years in Latin America and the Caribbean.

Suffrage had also been acquired by men through a gradual process in many countries. Their political rights, which were initially based on domicile and social and economic position, became more generally available. Women obtained the vote by a gradual process, but one which was occasionally quite different from that followed by men.

In many countries, the right to vote was first gained by women at the local level and only much later at the national level. For women, moreover, criteria other than gender had to be met before the right to vote was gained. Income level, education, marital status, occupation and race were all added considerations. At the end of the nineteenth century in Finland, Iceland and Sweden, for example, the franchise applied only to single women, as married women were considered to be under the

---

[6] The name was changed to Myanmar since June 1989

[7] Restricted to persons classified as white.

guardianship of their husbands.

In Belgium, a 1919 law gave the right to vote in national elections to the widows or mothers of servicemen killed during the war and citizens wounded or killed by the enemy. The same was true in Canada, where in 1917 women who were serving in the military or who had a close relative serving in the military were granted the right to vote at the federal level.

In Portugal, a law of 1931 gave women the right to vote, though they had to have completed secondary or higher studies whereas men only had to know how to read and write to be eligible to vote. In Bolivia, in 1938, literate women only were given the right to vote. In Egypt, where women's voting was voluntary, women were required to apply formally to vote, in sharp contrast to the automatic and obligatory character of male suffrage. The extra effort demanded of women resulted in few women actually registering to vote.

In countries under colonial rule, the process of according the right to vote was highly variable. In Kenya, for example, the right to vote was granted to European women in 1919, to African men and women who fulfilled certain conditions related to property and educational level in 1956, and only to all Kenyans in 1963. In Zimbabwe only men and British women could vote until 1957. That year saw the right to vote extended to black married women.[8] In order to be registered as a voter, a person had to have a specified level of income. These types of restriction are rare now.

THE RIGHT TO HOLD PUBLIC OFFICE, AND THE PRACTICE

Data compiled by the Inter-Parliamentary Union, provided by parliamentarians themselves and included in WISTAT, show that in most countries the right to vote and the right to stand for election were usually accorded at the same time. There were, however, a few countries, including the Netherlands, Norway and the United States, where the right to stand for election was given prior to the right to vote.

The case of the United States is illustrative. The Constitution of 1788 did not specify gender as a qualification for election to public office but rather referred to 'members' or 'persons'. As a result, in theory at least, women had the same right to stand for election as men. The same Constitution, however, initially restricted the right to vote to free males, and the right of women to vote in national elections was only accorded by constitutional amendment in 1920. However, in some states, women were given the right to vote at the subnational level earlier and women had been elected to state offices and even to the national parliament before 1920. One of these, Jeannette Rankin, who was elected to the Congress of the United States from the state of Wyoming in 1916, was the only member of that body to vote against the entry of the United States into the First World War.

---

[8] Inter-Parliamentary Union, Participation of Women in Political Life and in the Decision-making Process: A World Survey as at 1 April 1988, 'Reports and documents' series, No. 15 (Geneva, 1988) pp. 45-46.

There are also examples of countries where women were allowed to vote before they were allowed to hold public office. These include Canada (vote in 1917, public office in 1920), NewZealand (vote in 1893, public office in 1919), Peru (vote in 1950, public office in 1956), Syrian Arab Republic (vote in 1949, public office in 1953), Zaire (vote in 1967, public office in 1970) and Zimbabwe (vote in 1957, public office in 1978). However, it is doubtful that these differences affected women's chances to participate in public office over the longer term.

The right to hold office certainly did not mean that women would automatically do so, however. In slightly less than half of the 86 countries on which the Inter-Parliamentary Union has data, the first woman was elected to parliament the same year or within two years of the granting of the vote (see table 1). In many countries, however, there was an average delay of five years between the date that women were permitted to stand for election and the date that the first woman entered parliament.

Table 1. The gap between women's right to hold office and their first election to parliament

First parliamentarian (year unrestricted vote given)	Percentage of countries	Number of countries
Before	8.1	7
Same year	31.4	27
One or two years after	16.3	14
Three years or more after	44.2	38

Source: Inter-Parliamentary Union, Participation of Women in Political Life and in the Decision-making Process: A World Survey as at 1 April 1988 (Geneva, 1988), tables I and II.

The countries in which the first woman was elected to parliament before an unrestricted right to vote existed were mostly those in which women had previously had a limited right to vote. In some, this was based on property or other qualifications, as was the case of Norway, where the first woman was elected to parliament in 1911 even though unrestricted suffrage was only granted in 1913. In others it was based on the fact that some subnational jurisdictions (states or provinces) accorded the right to vote earlier, as was the case, already noted, in the United States.

Of the countries in which there was a large gap, the longest was Australia, where 65 years passed between gaining the vote and the election of the first woman to parliament. In only four countries for which the Inter-Parliamentary Union has information, where women had the vote, no woman had ever been elected to parliament (Djibouti, Jordan, Morocco and the United Arab Emirates).

In most countries the pattern was for at least one woman to be elected immediately upon the granting of the vote (frequently at independence), or within a few years. However, as discussed in chapter II, below, the fact that one woman was elected to parliament did not mean that others would follow.

INTERNATIONAL NORMS REGARDING THE PARTICIPATION OF WOMEN IN DECISION-MAKING

The right to vote and to hold public office are only the first steps. Women should not only have a right to participate in decision-making, but also public policy should encourage them to exercise that right. In the Convention on the Elimination of All Forms of Discrimination against Women, it is specified in article 7 that:

> States Parties shall take all appropriate measures to eliminate discrimination against women in the political and public life of the country and, in particular, shall ensure to women, on equal terms with men, the right:
> - To vote in all elections and public referenda and to be eligible for election to all publicly elected bodies;
> - To participate in the formulation of government policy and the implementation thereof and to hold public office and perform all public functions at all levels of government;
> - To participate in non-governmental organizations and associations concerned with the public and political life of the country.

As of 1 September 1991, the Convention had been ratified or acceded to by 108countries, and signed but not ratified by an additional 10 countries. For the 108 States parties to the Convention, it should be embodied in their national law.

The Nairobi Forward-looking Strategies for the Advancement of Women contain many affirmations of the need to involve women in decision-making. An entire section is devoted to equality in political participation and decision-making. It is stated:

> Governments and political parties should intensify efforts to stimulate and ensure equality of participation by women in all national and local legislative bodies and to achieve equity in the appointment, election and promotion of women to high posts in executive, legislative and judiciary branches in those bodies. ... (paragraph 86)

> Governments should effectively secure participation of women in the decision-making processes at a national, state and local level through legislative and administrative measures. ... Special activities should be undertaken to increase the

recruitment, nomination and promotion of women, especially to decision-making and policy-making positions, by publicizing posts more widely, increasing upward mobility and so on, until equitable representation of women is achieved. ... (paragraph 88)

Women should be an integral part of the process of defining the objectives and modes of development, as well as of developing strategies and measures for their implementation. The need for women to participate fully in political processes and to have an equal share of power in guiding development efforts and in benefiting from them should be recognized. ... (paragraph 111)

Women's equal role in decision-making with respect to peace and related issues-should be seen as one of their basic human rights and as such should be enhanced and encouraged at the national, regional and international levels. ... (paragraph 253)

Women should be able to participate actively in the decision-making process related to the promotion of international peace and co-operation. Governments should take the necessary measures to facilitate this participation by institutional, educational and organizational means. ... (paragraph 266)

Steps should be taken to increase the participation of women in international, regional and subregional level activities and decision-making, including those directly or indirectly concerned with the maintenance of peace and security, the role of women in development and the achievement of equality between women and men. (paragraph 313)

At the international level, there is a consensus that measures should be taken to ensure that the right to participate in decision-making is translated into practice. That is the issue for almost every country, and is the subject of this book.

CHAPTER II
WOMEN IN PARLIAMENT

The obvious place to look for women in decision-making at the national level is in parliaments. A parliament is a public body consisting of members elected or appointed to represent the interests of the people of the country. The role of the parliament in decision-making varies from country to country. In some, the boundary between the legislative and executive branches is not easy to draw since ministers are members of the parliament, which votes along party lines. When a parliamentary majority is lost, the Government changes. In others, a separation of powers exists and the role of the legislature, besides passing laws, is more of a watchdog on executive implementation. But in all systems, it is the parliament that represents the legitimacy of the Government, by reflecting the will of the people.

Parliaments, moreover, are a major source for the recruitment of the highest level decision makers. It is automatic in systems where ministers must be sitting members of parliament(MPs); it is a source of experienced people in others. If women are not among the members of parliaments who are elected by people, at least half of whom are also women, they are unlikely to be represented at executive decision-making levels. The issues to address are the number of women in parliament, what the trends and differences are, and why the level is low or high.

THE NUMBER OF WOMEN IN PARLIAMENT

In many countries, parliaments consist of a single house and are termed unicameral. In others, parliaments are bicameral, and consist of two separate parts, usually termed an upper and a lower chamber. The actual names vary according to national tradition and history. In the United Kingdom, the upper chamber is the House of Lords, the lower, the House of Commons. In France, Italy, Poland and the United States, the upper chamber is called the Senate.

In bicameral parliaments, the powers of the chambers can be quite distinct and the upper chamber is usually less powerful than the lower. In many countries, the members of the upper chamber are appointed or enter by heredity (e.g. the House of

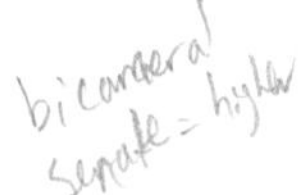

Lords in the United Kingdom). In others, with federal systems, the upper house is elected indirectly by provincial bodies (e.g. the German Bundesrat). In yet others, although directly elected, the upper house has fewer powers (e.g. the House of Councillors in Japan). However, in some countries, the upper house has co-equal powers (e.g. the Senate of the United States or of Poland).

In order to permit a direct comparison across different systems, the present analyses are largely based on the percentage of the total seats obtained by women in the single or lower chamber. This can be justified by the fact that there are few major differences between the representation of women and men in upper or lower chambers in those countries where the powers of the two are equivalent, while in other countries the role of the upper chamber is less important. Thus, when the text refers to women in parliament, unless otherwise indicated, it refers to women in single or lower chambers.

For most countries, the available data pertain to elections held between 1985 and 1987 and are based on the results of the elections. They do not take into account changes which might have occurred following resignations or by-elections. Data is not available on women's parliamentary participation for 31 of the 155 countries used in the analysis, either because no parliament existed or because the existing parliament was in suspension. Of the total, 17 countries (11 per cent) had no legislature based on election in 1987. These are Bahrain, BruneiDarussalam, Burkina Faso, Central African Republic, Chad, Ghana, Guinea, Haiti, Kuwait, Lesotho, Mauritania, Niger, Nigeria, Oman, Qatar, Saudi Arabia and the United Arab Emirates.[9] Of these, only 5 - Brunei Darussalam, Oman, Qatar, Saudi Arabia and the United Arab Emirates - have never had an institution which could be described as a popular assembly. The other 12 countries either had an established assembly which was currently suspended by a military regime or a transitional Government that was working on a new constitution.[10]

In 1987, in the 124 countries with parliaments for which data are available, an average of 9.7 per cent of the members of the single or lower chamber were women (see table 2). The averages were lower for developing regions than for developed. The average percentage was particularly high in Eastern Europe although, as will be shown below, that figure is outdated. There was little difference between the average figures in the developing regions.

---

[9] The United Arab Emirates had a legislative body whose members were all nominated, rather than popularly elected.

[10] D. Derbyshire and I. Derbyshire, Political Systems of the World, (Edinburgh, Chambers, 1989), p. 68; see also Inter-Parliamentary Union, op. cit., p. 58.

Table 2. Average percentage of women in lower houses or single chamber parliaments, 1987

Region	Average percentage of women	Number of countries
Africa	7.2	36
Asia and the Pacific	7.0	27
Latin America and the Caribbean	7.5	29
Western industrialized	13.2	23
Eastern Europe	26.6	9
All countries	9.7	124

The averages should not be taken to imply homogeneity among the different countries within and between regions. There is considerable variation between countries as shown in figure II, which uses a boxplot to indicate the difference.

Figure II. The boxplot

A boxplot is based on the median (the point below which half of the cases fall), the twenty-fifth and the seventy-fifth percentiles and values that are far removed from the rest. In figure II, the lower boundary of the box is the value that marks where the lowest 25 per cent of the countries begin, while the upper boundary is the value above which are the highest 25 per cent of the countries. That means that 50 per cent of all countries have values within the box. The asterisk in the box represents the median. In general a boxplot includes two categories of countries with especially high or low values. Countries with exceptionally high or low values are called "extremes" and are designated with the letter E. Countries with high or low values are called "outliers" and are designated with the letter O.

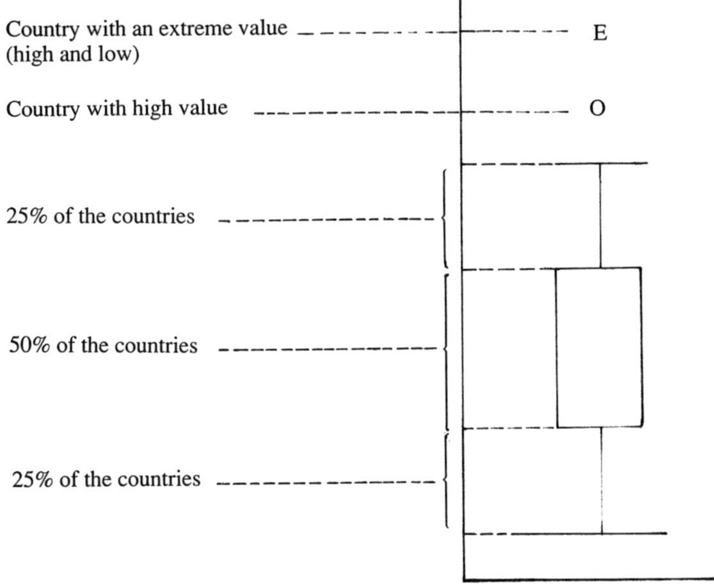

The variation between the countries in the proportion of women in parliament is shown in figure III. The lowest value is 0 per cent. Some 13 countries that have parliaments and have reported on gender composition to the Inter-Parliamentary Union, had no women among the members of their lower chambers. These included Antigua and Barbuda, Comoros, Djibouti, Jordan, Lebanon, Morocco, Papua New Guinea, Solomon Islands, Tonga, United Arab Emirates, Uruguay, Vanuatu and Yemen.

The highest level of 34.5 per cent was found in Norway, Romania and in the Union of Soviet Socialist Republics. The composition at the top proved to be transitory, since new elections reduced the percentage of women in both Romania and the Soviet Union. However, elections in Finland in April 1991 gave that country the honour of having the highest percentage of women in parliament, with a figure of 38.4 per cent.

Finland %

The 'middle' 50 per cent of the countries concerned lie between 3.7 per cent and 13.5 per cent. The nine outliers (the countries with relatively high scores) come from two recognizable groups: four Scandinavian countries, and four Eastern European countries and Cuba.

Figure III. Percentage of women in parliament, 1987

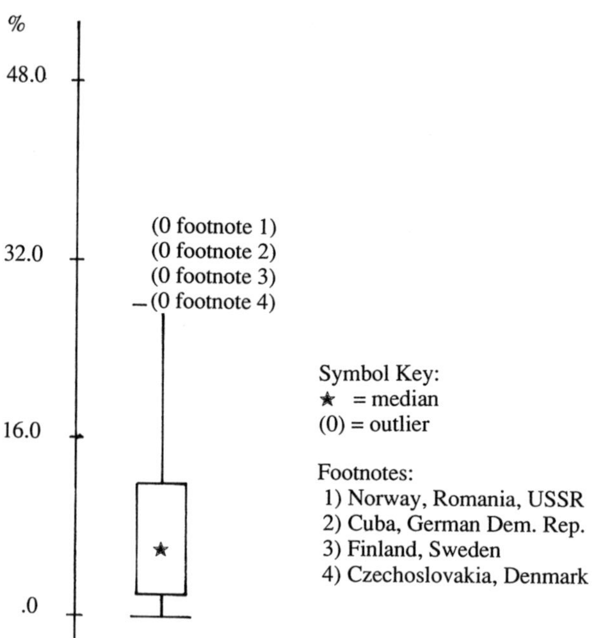

Region is a major factor, even for developing countries. The similar averages for Africa, Asia and the Pacific, and Latin America and the Caribbean mask great differences (see figure IV). More countries in Asia and the Pacific are below the average, for example. Moreover, despite the high average for Western industrialized countries, most of the countries in the group are not very dissimilar from those in Africa, and in Latin America and the Caribbean. The figures on Western industrialized countries are greatly affected by the Scandinavian countries, all of which have high percentages of women in parliament, in which the average figure reached 29.3 in 1987. Why women are so well-represented in Scandinavia needs detailed analysis. The very high level of representation of women in parliament in Eastern Europe in 1987 is discussed below.

Figure IV. Percentage of women in parliament, 1987

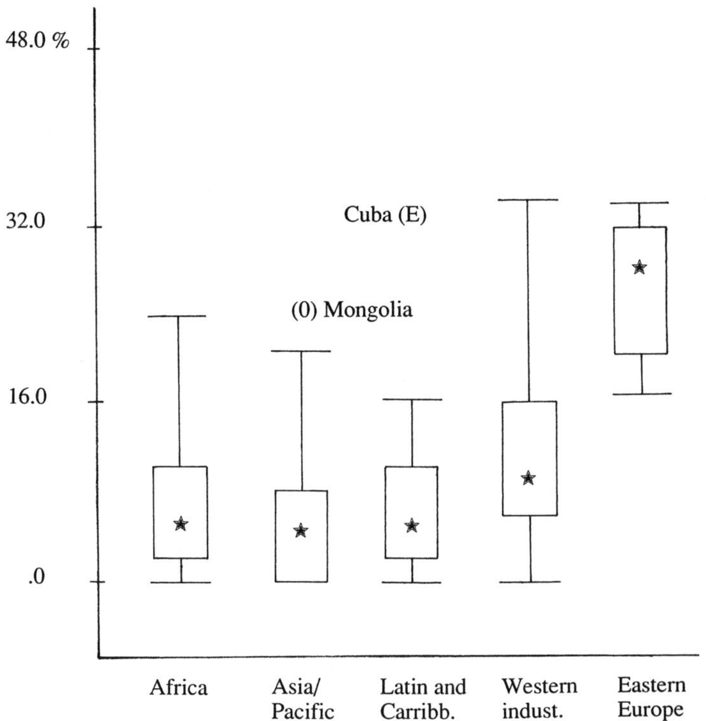

Key: ★ = Median (0) = Outlier (E) = Extreme

The countries in which there are no women in parliament have already been noted. They affect the statistics of those regions, such as Asia and the Pacific, Africa and Latin America and the Caribbean, where these situations tend to cluster.

Classifying countries according to whether they have a low, average or high proportion of women in parliament provides a sense of how national experiences converge in countries of the same geographical and cultural areas. Subregions can help to show this. It can be noted that the averages for North Africa, Southern Africa, Western Asia and South America all fall below 5 per cent. Subregions where the averages range between 5 and 12 per cent include West, Central and East Africa; South and South-east Asia and the Pacific, Central America, Southern Europe and North America. Subregions with averages over 12 per cent include east Asia, the Caribbean, West and Northern Europe and Eastern Europe.

Information exists for 73 countries on the proportion of women in parliament in

1975 and 1987. (For the other 90 countries, either no parliament existed in one of the periods, or information by gender was not reported.) By 1987, a general trend was apparent: the proportion of women in parliament worldwide had increased since 1975. The average improvement in representation was 3.8 per cent. The largest reported improvement was registered by Romania, with an increase of 19.2 per cent over the period, and by Norway, with an increase of 18.9 per cent. In contrast, Hungary showed a decline of 7.8 per cent during the period, and Zaire a fall of 7.5 per cent.

These averages, however, mask considerable variation. In general, with the exception of Western industrialized countries, the average increase in other regions has not been greatly different (see figure V). In Africa, there was an increase of 2.3 per cent, in Latin America of 3.9 per cent, in Asia and the Pacific of 1.8 per cent and in Eastern Europe of 2.5 per cent. However, while in all regions there are countries that have improved greatly, improved slightly or not improved at all, there are regional differences (see table 3). Most Western industrialized countries have seen a relatively large increase in women in parliament. In contrast, in Asia and the Pacific, only one country, the Syrian Arab Republic, had an increase in the high range (6.5 per cent improvement). In Africa, almost half of the countries reporting had either no change or negative change.

Figure V. Change in the percentage of women in parliament, 1975-1987

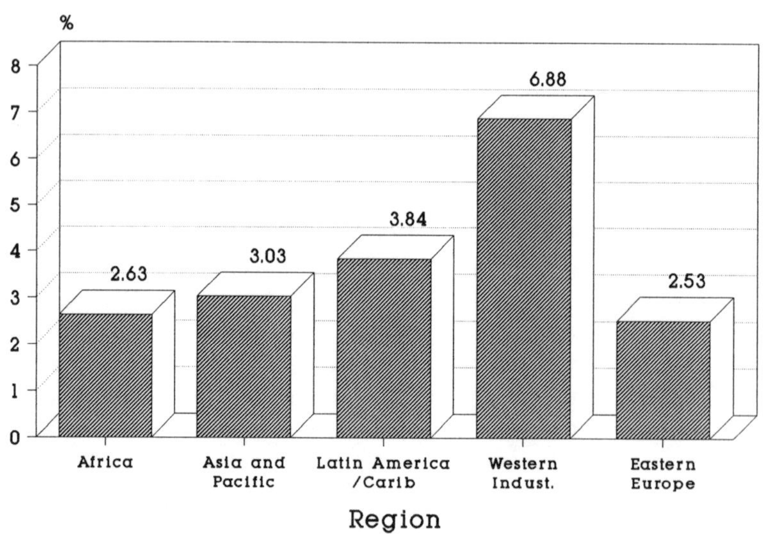

Table 3. Type of change in the proportion of women in parliament, 1975 to 1987

Type of change	Africa	Latin America and the Caribbean	Asia and the Pacific	Western industrialized Countries	Eastern Europe
High positive (>6 per cent)	26.7	33.3	6.3	57.1	11.1
Low positive to average (1 per cent - 6 per cent)	26.7	41.7	62.4	28.6	66.7
No change or negative (0 - 8 per cent)	46.7	25.0	31.3	14.3	22.2
Total	100	100	100	100	100
Number of countries	15	12	16	21	9

By far the highest average participation of women in parliament in 1987 was in the Eastern European countries. With 26.6 per cent, their average was twice as high as the Western industrialized countries and well above the average for all countries. However, with the exception of Yugoslavia, national elections have been held since 1988 in all Eastern European countries as part of political and economic reform. One result has been that the proportion of women in parliament in that region has declined precipitously in every country (see table 4). The new figures place countries in that region at about the world average.

Table 4. Percentage of women in a lower house or single chamber of parliament in Eastern European countries, 1988 and 1990-1991

Country	1988	1990-1991
Albania	28.8	6.2
Bulgaria	21.0	8.5
Czecholslovakia	29.5	6.0
German Democratic Republic	32.2	20.5
Hungary	20.9	7.0
Poland	20.2	13.3
Romania	34.4	3.5
USSR	34.5	15.6
Yugoslavia	17.7	17.7
Average	27.5	10.9

The reasons for this are complex, but one of the factors can be that in the new political systems the importance of the parliament increased, in the sense that it had more power than before. Hence, a seat in parliament is more important. The previous political system had provided for parliamentary representation on a quota basis for a wide range of occupational and social groups, including women, with the intention of maintaining a parliament which essentially represented a cross-section of the population. The increase in the importance of the parliament meant that it would more accurately reflect the real power in society. In that sense, paradoxically, in Eastern European countries, more democratization in political decision-making has been accompanied by reduced female representation with regard to men.

The average percentage of women parliamentarians for an area gives no information on the variance within that group of countries. Clearly, there is intraregional variability, most notably in the Western industrialized countries. The average percentage of women in parliament in 1987 in the Nordic countries was 29.3 per cent, but in other Western industrialized countries was only 9.9 per cent, which was not much higher than the average for developing countries of 7 per cent.

These figures call into question, at least for parliamentary representation, any assumption of a strong relationship between economic development and the existence of democratic systems. There is no strong relationship between development measured in terms of national income and democracy measured in terms of women's representation. The World Bank for its purposes classifies countries according to national income. Countries classified by the World Bank as low income developing countries (annual per capita income below $US 545 in 1988) included China, Bangladesh, Ethiopia, India, Pakistan, Rwanda, Sudan and Zambia. Developing countries with a middle-level income (annual per capita income between $US 546 and $US 2,160) included Bolivia, Cameroon, Honduras, Mauritania, Nigeria, Philippines, Thailand and Zimbabwe. Developing countries with an upper-middle level of annual per capita income (between $US 2,161 and $US 5,420) included Argentina, Brazil, Greece, Hungary, Malaysia, Oman, Portugal, Singapore and Venezuela.

The results of applying the classification of low, middle and upper-middle income to developing countries, and adding the distinctions within industrialized countries between Eastern European, Nordic and other Western industrialized countries, are shown in table 5 in terms of the percentage of women in parliament in 1987.

Table 5. Average percentage of women in parliament, 1987

Group of countries	Number of countries	Average percentage of women in parliament
Developing countries:		
Low income	30	7.6
Middle income	35	5.9
Upper-middel income	21	9.5
Developed countries:		
Nordic	5	29.3
Eastern Europe	9	26.6
Other Western industrialized	16	9.9

The average representation of women in the parliaments of petroleum-exporting countries, such as Algeria, Angola, Brunei–Darussalam, Indonesia, Iran (Islamic Republic of), Iraq, Mexico and Venezuela, is 8.6 per cent. The average for countries included in the World Bank's category of major developing country exporters of manufactures, such as Argentina, Brazil, Republic of Korea and Singapore, is 4.6 per cent. The countries in Asia with centrally planned economies, as a subgroup, have an average of 21.2 per cent.

In the upper chambers of those countries that had bicameral parliaments, in 1987 the average percentage of women members was 10.1, not significantly different than for lower chambers. Only in Latin America and the Caribbean was the percentage higher than for lower chambers, but the difference was slight (9.1 compared with

7.5 per cent).

In sum, the representation of women in parliament, although increasing slowly, is still low. Indeed, in terms of the target of 30 per cent by 1995 set by the Economic and Social Council of the United Nations for women in parliament, political parties, trade unions and interest associations, only eight countries had reached that level in their parliaments by 1987. Of those, four (Czechoslovakia, German Democratic Republic, Romania and the Soviet Union) had reverted to much lower levels by 1990. Only three Nordic countries (Finland, Norway and Sweden) and Cuba were still above the targeted level in 1990. If progress were to continue at the present rate, it would be well into the twenty-first century before even the 1995 targets were met, let alone the goal of equality.

WOMEN IN PARLIAMENT IN 16 SELECTED COUNTRIES

The case-studies prepared for the Expert Group Meeting on Equality in Political Participation and Decision-making, held at Vienna in 1989, provide a greater sense of the flavour of what has been happening at the national level. Most of the situations, regionally and structurally, contained in the global statistics are reflected in the 16 countries represented at the meeting. The percentage of women in the upper and lower houses of the parliaments of the 16 countries at the time of the meeting are shown in table 6.

Table 6. Right to vote and percentage of women in the lower and upper houses of parliament, 1989

Country	Year of unrestricted right to vote	Women in lower house		Women in upper house	
		(%)	Year	(%)	Year
Algeria	1962	2.4	1986	a/	
Austria	1918	11.5	1986	22.4	1986
Costa Rica	1949	10.0	1986	a/	
France	1944	5.0	1989	3.0	1989
Greece	1952	4.3	1989	a/	
India	1950	7.9	1984	11.4	1987
Japan	1945	1.4	1989	13.1	1989
Netherlands	1919	25.0	1989	26.0	1989
Philippines	1937	9.0	1989	8.6	1989
Poland	1918	13.5	1989	6.0	1989
Spain	1931	8.4	1989	a/	
Sweden	1921	37.8	1988	a/	
United Republic of Tanzania	1959	10.2	1985	a/	
United States	1920	5.3	1986	2.0	1986
USSR	1917	20.0	1989	a/	1988
Venezuela	1947	11.7	1988	6.8	

a/ Having a unicameral parliament.

Source: Inter-Parliamentary Union, Participation of Women in Political Life and in the Decision-making Process: A World Survey as at 1 April 1988, series 'Reports and documents', No. 15, Geneva, 1988, table I; and case-studies prepared for the Expert Group Meeting on Equality in Political Participation and Decision-making, Vienna, 18-22 September 1989 (EGM/EPPDM/1989/CS.1-18).

Algeria

Algeria became independent in 1962 after an armed struggle in which many women participated. The current Constitution was adopted in 1976 and amended in 1979. A socialist democratic and popular republic was created, with the National Liberation Front(FLN) as the single political party. Under the Constitution, FLN nominated the President, who was then elected by popular vote. There was a single chamber assembly of 295 deputies, all nominees of FLN elected by a simple plurality voting system.

In 1989, a referendum on a revision to the Constitution to allow for pluralized politics resulted in overwhelming support for change. Equal rights had been guaranteed by the Constitution, which stated: 'All political, economic, social and cultural rights of the Algerian woman are guaranteed by the Constitution.' The revised Constitution stated that citizens were equal before the law without any discrimination on the basis of sex, opinion or other personal or social circumstance.

Algerian women first entered the assembly in 1962. Since then, the representation of women in the assembly has been rather low. In 1979, 10 (3.4 per cent) women were elected, but in 1986 this number again decreased to 7 (2.4 per cent). A larger number of women have been elected at the municipal level.

Austria

Austria has a two-chamber federal assembly, consisting of a National Council (Nationalrat) with 183 members elected by universal adult suffrage by a party list system of proportional representation, and a Federal Council (Bundesrat) with 63 members, who are indirectly elected by the provincial assemblies.

In 1918, when women attained the right to vote and to be elected for the first time, 10 women were elected to the lower house, so they held approximately 6 per cent of the total 170 seats. The patterns of gender distribution in the parliament remained similar after the Second World War. This situation began to change in the 1970s. In 1975, women held more than 7 per cent of the seats in the lower house for the first time in the history of the Second Republic. In subsequent years, the number of women in parliament continued to increase, and in 1983 they exceeded 10 per cent for the first time. In 1986, 21 women were elected, which represented 11.5 per cent of the total of 183 seats. In the most recent election, in October 1990, the figure increased to 20 per cent, with most parties increasing their proportion of women. The Socialist Party includes a higher percentage of women than the other parties.

The upper house of Parliament in Austria, while having the power to initiate, enact and reject legislation, rarely makes use of its constitutional powers. The representation of women in the upper house is considerably greater than in the lower house: since 1970 it has fluctuated between 16 and 28 per cent. One explanation advanced for the higher representation of women in this body is its relative lack of importance.

Costa Rica

In Costa Rica there is a popularly elected President and a single-chamber assembly consisting of 57 members elected through a party list system of proportional representation. The Constitution of 1949 guarantees equal rights for men, women and minorities, and discrimination is explicitly prohibited. It includes the right to vote, the right for women to be elected to political office and other political participation. However, throughout its history, and not even since 1949 when women were legally given their political rights, very few women have reached high decision-making positions in Costa Rica. In 1953, three women were elected to Congress, followed by two women in 1958, one in 1962, three in 1966, four in 1970 and three in 1974. In 1989, five women (10 per cent) occupied seats in the Congress.

France

France has a two-chamber parliament. It comprises the National Assembly, with 577 members elected from single-member constituencies on the basis of a two-ballot, absolute majority system, and the Senate, with 321 members who are indirectly elected by an electoral college composed of members from several political bodies.

The political representation of women has always been very low, especially compared with other Western European countries such as Austria, the Netherlands and Sweden. One explanation is the difference in voting systems, which is explained in a later chapter. In 1945, the lower house of France included 6.7 per cent women. Since then, this figure has not been exceeded. In 1980, 3.6 per cent members of the National Assembly and 2.3 per cent of the Senate were women. Nine years later these figures had changed little. In 1989, only 5 per cent of the National Assembly were women. In the Senate, the percentage of women was even lower at 3 per cent.

Greece

The President of Greece is elected by the parliament. This parliament consists of one chamber with 300 members, all elected by universal adult suffrage, through a party-list system of proportional representation.

In the 30-year period from 1958-1988, women's representation in the parliament of Greece increased fourfold. The major increase occurred only after 1977. The only increase in the immediate post-war years was from one to three women, but during the 1980s, it was from 10 to 13 women. For example, in the elections of 1981, half of the women candidates of the Panhellenic Socialist Organization (PASOK) (the largest party) and more than one third of those of New Democracy (the second largest party) were elected, although women represented only 4.8 per cent of the candidates of PASOK and 2.6 per cent of the candidates of New Democracy. After the election of 1989, the percentage of women parliamentarians was 4.3.

India

India is a federal republic composed of 25 self-governing states, each with a legislative assembly. The President is elected by an electoral college, composed of members from both the federal and the state assemblies. The federal assembly is a two-chamber body, comprising a 544-member lower house (Lok Sabha), whose members are directly elected from single-member constituencies by universal adult suffrage. The upper house (Raj Sabha) has 245 members, who are indirectly elected by state assemblies on a regional quota basis.

Both men and women fought against British rule. Voices were raised for the first time advocating the women's cause, leading to the abolition of child marriage, and supporting women's education and the remarrying of widows. An examination of women's political participation shows that the number of women elected to the representative bodies has been increasing, although the number of women who are elected is still very small. In 1952, 4 per cent of the seats in the lower house were occupied by women; in 1984 it was about 8 per cent. The representation of women in the upper house has been slightly higher. In 1987, there were 11.4 per cent women senators.

Japan

The Japanese Diet is a two-chamber body, composed of a 252-member upper house (House of Councillors) and a 512-member lower house (House of Representatives). The upper house has 152 members elected from 47 prefectural constituencies on the basis of the limited vote system and 100 elected nationally by proportional representation. Members of the lower house are also elected on the basis of the 'limited vote'.[11]

Japanese women obtained the right to vote and to be elected in 1945 and exercised it for the first time in April 1946 at the general elections for the House of Representatives. At that time, 39 women were elected, giving them 8 per cent of the seats. This, however, was an all-time high. In the second general election, only 15 women were elected (3 per cent). In the period 1975-1986, the number of female members never exceeded 11 (2.4 per cent) in the lower house and 22 (8.8 per cent) in the upper house. After the 1990 elections, the percentage of women in the upper house is 13.1 per cent and in the lower house 1.4 per cent. On a combined basis, the overall percentage of women in the Diet is 5.3 per cent. Women have done slightly better in the upper house, which may be related to the fact that it is less

---

[11] Electors cast a single vote and the candidates with the highest number of votes in each single- or multi-member constituency are elected on the basis of the rank-order of votes received. Electors are given an additional, separate vote for 100 additional members. (See D. Derbyshire and I. Derbyshire, 'Political Systems of the World' (Edinburgh, Chambers, 1989), p. 635.

influential than the lower house.

Netherlands
The Netherlands is a constitutional and hereditary monarchy. Since 1890, the Head of State has been a woman. It has a two-chamber assembly, a Second (lower) Chamber of 150 members and a First (upper) Chamber of 75 members. The representatives of the Second Chamber are elected by universal adult suffrage, by a party list system of proportional representation. The senators are indirectly elected by representatives of the Provincial Councils.

Women's suffrage was introduced in 1919. However, this did not lead to proportional representation of women and men. Before the Second World War, the percentage of women in the Second Chamber never exceeded 7 per cent. In the First Chamber, women's representation was even lower: not more than two women were seated in this body. The percentage of women representatives in the Second Chamber increased gradually after the Second World War, but until the 1970s it was still less than 10 per cent. As in other Western industrialized countries, the women's movement during the late 1960s and 1970s had an effect on the number of women in decision-making bodies. Since then, the percentage has increased steadily. After the 1989 elections, women accounted for 25 per cent of the seats in the Second Chamber and 26 per cent of the seats in the First Chamber.

Philippines
In the Philippines, the President works in tandem with a two-chamber legislature. The Senate is made up of 24 members directly elected by universal adult suffrage. The House of Representatives consists of a maximum of 250 members, 200 of whom are directly elected at the district level, with the remaining 50 appointed by the President.

In 1991, the President of the Philippines was Corazon Aquino, a woman, who had been in office since 1986. She was an exception, since very few women have run for public office, especially when it requires active campaigning on a national scale.

The percentage of women parliamentarians in the Philippines has never exceeded 10. Only one woman was elected to each House of the Congress between 1946 and 1961. In 1961, two women were elected to the House of Representatives. This number increased to 6 in 1965, decreased to 3 in 1969, and in 1989 increased again to 18 women (7.2 per cent). In 1989, 2 out of 23 members of the Senate were women (8.6 per cent). Slightly more women could be found in the lower house, where campaigning is confined to specified localities, as compared with the Senate, where candidates have to campaign all over the country. Women seem to have become more active in politics, especially in the last three years of the Aquino administration, and having a woman President is said to have helped to open a pathway for women in politics.

Poland
Poland has a two-chamber legislature, made up of a 460-member lower assembly

and a 100-member upper chamber, the Senate. After the parliamentary reforms which included re-instating the upper chamber and holding partly free elections with fixed quotas for various political forces, as a temporary compromise in 1989, the composition of parliament was as follows: 253 of the seats of the lower chamber were reserved for contests between candidates of the Communist Party and its allies, 46 seats for a national list of dignitaries and the remaining 161 seats for non-communist party candidates. To be elected, candidates needed to secure an absolute majority of valid votes in the first run. There were no quotas for election to the Senate.

Women attained the right to vote and to stand for election immediately after Poland regained independence in 1918. However, these rights did not automatically lead to the appearance of women in politics. Women constituted only 2 per cent of the members of the lower chamber and 5 per cent of the upper chamber in the period preceding the outbreak of the Second World War. In the 10 successive terms following the adoption of a new constitution in 1952, women held from 19 to 106 out of 460 seats in the lower chamber. Their number never exceeded a quarter of the total number of seats. In the early 1980s, when the opposition intensified its action and the Solidarity trade union took the form of a mass movement, women comprised 23 per cent of the total of the members of parliament, the highest proportion in the history of the Polish parliament. In the succeeding election, women won 20.2 per cent of the seats. After the election in 1989, the percentage of women declined to 13.4 per cent, one of the lowest proportions since the war, and in the Senate the proportion only reached 6 per cent.

Spain

The 1978 Constitution of Spain established a constitutional monarchy, with a hereditary king as formal Head of State. The National Assembly consists of two chambers, the Congress of Deputies, with 350 members and the Senate with up to 257 members. Deputies are elected by universal adult suffrage by a party-list system of proportional representation. Of the senators, 208 are directly elected to represent the whole country and 49 are appointed to represent the regions.

Spain was one of the last countries in Europe to grant women the right to vote. Although the new constitution adopted in 1931 after the fall of the monarchy provided universal suffrage for all citizens over the age of 23, when the Nationalists won the civil war in 1939, those rights were abolished. General Franco established laws which rescinded divorce, abortion, coeducation, the right to work and the right to strike. Women were expected to stay at home and produce children. Universal suffrage was only re-established in 1977.

When the first democratic elections since 1936 took place in 1977, of 350 deputies only 21 women (6 per cent) were elected. Women were elected in 14 of the 52 electoral districts. Fewer women were elected in the most sparsely populated provinces than in provinces with large cities. After the 1989 elections, the percentage of women deputies increased from 2 to 8.4 per cent. Women's representation in the Senate has always been lower than in the Congress of Deputies. In 1977, only

2.4 per cent of those elected to the Senate were women, in 1982, 4.3 per cent and in 1986, 5.5 per cent.

Sweden
Sweden is a constitutional hereditary monarchy with a king as formal Head of State. The parliament consists of a single-chamber assembly (Riksdag) of 349 members elected by universal adult suffrage by a party-list system of proportional representation.

Sweden is one of the countries where women obtained the vote at the beginning of the twentieth century. The overall trend there has been for women's representation in parliament to increase. Over a 20-year period, the proportion of women in parliament rose from 13 per cent in 1966/67 to 31 per cent in 1986/87. Between 1970 and 1973, women's representation increased by 50 per cent. That increase may have been partly due to the emergence of feminism at the time. After the election in 1988, the female representation of the Riksdag reached 37.8 per cent. There is now a commonly accepted norm in Sweden that the lesser-represented sex should not have less than 40 per cent.

Union of Soviet Socialist Republics
Under the 1977 Constitution, the Union of Soviet Socialist Republics is a federal State comprising 15 constituent union republics. Each of these union republics has a single-chamber assembly and a government. Prior to the constitutional reforms of 1988-1989, the highest organ of the central Government had traditionally been the Supreme Soviet, a two-chamber assembly, each chamber comprising 750 members, elected by universal adult suffrage from a single list of candidates approved by the Communist Party of the Soviet Union. The upper chamber was called the Soviet of Nationalities. Under the constitutional reforms of 1989 the old Supreme Soviet was replaced by a new Congress of Peoples' Deputies, with 2,250 members. As before, 750 members are elected from territorial constituencies and 750 from national-territorial constituencies. For these seats, competition between candidates approved by selection committees has been introduced. The remaining 750 seats are allocated between 32 officially recognized social organizations, one of which is the Soviet Women's Association. The members of the new Supreme Soviet are elected from the members of the Congress of Peoples' Deputies.

The Soviet Union was one of the first countries where women were granted the vote, in 1917. After the Second World War, the representation of women in the Soviet of Nationalities was, compared with the other countries, the highest, ranging between 23 per cent in 1950 and 35 per cent in 1984. However, in 1989, the share of women in the new Congress dropped to 20 per cent.

United Republic of Tanzania
The United Republic of Tanzania became independent from British rule in December 1961. Under its constitution, the United Republic of Tanzania is a one-party State, and the President is chosen by the Party. There is a single-chamber assembly

of up to 231 members. Of the parliamentarians, 101 are elected by universal adult suffrage by a simple plurality voting system for the mainland. The rest are similarly elected for the islands of Zanzibar and Pemba or nominated by the party and President. Fifteen seats are reserved for women. During the struggles for independence, Tanzanian women played a very active role as party members, supporters and activists who mobilized support for the struggle for independence. In 1961, 7.5 per cent of the members of parliament were women. In 1980, the participation rate had increased to 10.7 per cent. In the present Union Governmental Parliament of the United Republic of Tanzania, there are 25 women members of parliament (10.2 per cent).

United States of America

The United States of America is a federal republic comprising 50 states and the District of Columbia. At the head of the executive branch of Government is a President, elected by electors who are chosen by universal adult suffrage. The Congress consists of a 435-member House of Representatives and a 100-member Senate. The senators are elected, two from each state, on a state-wide basis. The representatives are elected from single-member constituencies, distributed by state according to population.

In 1920, the Nineteenth Amendment to the Constitution of the United States granted women the right to vote. Since the Second World War, women's representation in the federal legislature has not exceeded 6 per cent. In the Senate, there have on average been two women members over the period, with a maximum of three. In the House, the number has grown from 7 in 1948 (1.6 per cent) to 23 in 1986 (5.3 per cent). In 1989, women held 28 seats in the federal legislature, amounting to 6 per cent of the House and 2 per cent of the Senate. The representation of women at state level is, however, somewhat better. In 1988, women held 15.8 per cent of all the seats of the state legislatures, a four-fold increase since 1969. With regard to the state executives, in 1988 women held 40 (12.1 per cent) of the 330 elective executive offices at the state level, including three governors, five lieutenant governors, 11 secretaries of state and 9 state treasurers.

Venezuela

The 1961 Constitution of Venezuela provides for a President, who is Head of State and Head of Government, and a two-chamber National Congress, consisting of a Senate and a Chamber of Deputies. The Senate has 44 members elected by universal adult suffrage on the basis of two representatives for each state. The Chamber of Deputies has 196 deputies, also elected by universal adult suffrage, by a party-list system of proportional representation.

In Venezuela, women obtained a restricted vote in 1945, but in 1947 women received the universal right to elect and to be elected. The Constitution of 1961 established that no discrimination in politics was allowed on the grounds of race, sex, beliefs or social condition.

In 1948, 4.5 per cent of the senators and 1.9 per cent of the deputies elected were women. With the exception of 1953, when the percentage of women in the lower house rose to 10, there has been little change in these proportions. However, there has been a slow but steady increase, and in 1988 there were three women senators (6.8 per cent) and 23 women representatives (11.7 per cent).

Comparative perspectives
Given the variety of political systems, comparisons must be made with care. In the countries covered in the case-studies two voting systems are widely used: the simple plurality voting system (Algeria, India, Philippines, United Republic of Tanzania and United States) and the list system based on proportional representation (Austria, Costa Rica, Greece, Netherlands, Spain and Venezuela). France, Poland and the Soviet Union use a second ballot. Under that system, a simple majority election is held and if no one achieves more than 50 per cent of the total vote, a second election is held. Only Japan uses a unique voting system: the limited vote. Countries also differ in political ideology and the number of parties. However, some conclusions can be drawn from the comparison of the case-study countries:

- As in the global statistical analysis, the highest percentages of women representatives are found in the European countries, followed by Latin America, Africa and Asia. Sweden has the highest percentage of women in parliament and Japan the lowest;

- In most of the countries studied, the representation of women in the upper house is on average lower than that in the lower house. However, in Austria, Japan and the Netherlands more women were seated in the upper chamber;

- Except for Japan and two Eastern European countries (Poland and the Soviet Union) the proportion of women representatives is slowly increasing.

WHY SO FEW?

The underrepresentation of women in positions of political power is a worldwide phenomenon. In describing the participation of women in parliament, some suggestions have already been made of possible explanations for this underrepresentation. For example, by comparing regions, differences between the more industrialized and less industrialized countries appear. The decreasing participation rates of women in several Eastern European countries have been discussed in relation to recent ideological and political changes. Finally, the voting system, the importance of the chamber and the year that women gained the right to vote have been suggested as possible factors influencing the likelihood of women entering politics.

The possible barriers to women's parliamentary participation can be examined more systematically using the information presented in the case-studies. Based on empirical studies of the recruitment and selection of women parliamentarians, a theoretical model of factors which help or hinder women to enter high political decision-making is suggested.

The presence of women in national parliaments is one of the clearest indicators of women's participation in political processes. This is closely linked to their participation in political parties and the role of women in parliamentary elections, as both voters and candidates.

Women constitute half of the population and so, in those countries with no restrictions on suffrage, at least half of the electorate. Voting in general elections is one of the easiest acts of participation. Earlier studies on voting behaviour show a gap between women and men in turnout in parliamentary elections. Men went more often to the polling booth than women.[12] There are still countries where fewer women than men vote, such as India, but there are also countries where women are slightly more likely to vote than men, as Japan, the Philippines and Sweden. Generally it appears that women exercise their right to vote in the same numbers as men.

Political participation should not be seen as restricted to participation in parties or representative bodies. Many women and men are involved in community action groups, in issue or interest groups, such as environmental or peace groups and women's organizations, or in individual political activities. Examples of the latter are canvassing, contacting civil servants or politicians, making calls to the media, joining in demonstrations or signing petitions. Although there is some evidence that women participate on the same level as men in what might be termed 'protest activities' or 'ad hoc activities', the majority of the participation studies all report the same result: men are more likely to be active in politics than women, especially when in the more conventional forms of political participation.[13]

One of these conventional activities is membership of a political party. This is often a precondition for becoming a representative in legislative bodies. Depending on the voting system, the political party plays a prominent role in the selection of candidates for elective office. This is particularly the case in countries where the party nominates the representatives, or in countries where a list system is used in combination with proportional representation. Recruitment is, in these cases, from the active members of the party. Generally not many citizens belong to a political party. In those countries where party membership is an economic or social asset, large numbers of people become active members. In the Netherlands, for example, only 4 per cent of the electorate are members of a political party. Little information is available on gender differences in the membership of political parties. However, where data exist, they show a lower membership rate for women than for men.

---

[12] See, for example, H. Tingsten, 'Political Behaviour: Studies in Election Statistics' (London, P.S. King, 1937); and M. Duverger, 'The Political Role of Women' (Paris, UNESCO, 1955).

[13] For an overview of factors influencing political participation, see Lester W. Milbrath and M. L. Goel, 'Political Participation: How and why do People get Involved in Politics' (Chicago, Rand McNally, 1977).

Moreover, it appears that not every party member can be considered as an activist, by which is meant those who go to party meetings, discuss party matters, become a member of a (local) party committee or participate in the selection of the candidates for elective office. Fewer women than men participate in an active way in a party.

Ironically, in many countries although fewer women than men stand for election, the proportion of women who get elected is larger than the proportion standing as candidates (E/CN.6/1989/7). However, taking all factors together, throughout the world, women are either absent or very poorly represented at the top of the political pyramid. At every stage of the process, the proportion of women involved becomes smaller. One way of explaining this vanishing act is to examine each step on the pathway to a seat in parliament.

PATHWAYS TO POWER

The path leading to a high-level political position is summarized below.

The first step is to be eligible for office. Those eligible for positions of political power are in most countries identified in the national constitution, which outlines conditions such as minimum age, citizenship, the number of years resident in the country, not having lost the right to vote, or similar provisions.

The next step is the process termed recruitment, which narrows the number of potential politicians. It is the process by which people become involved in political, especially party, activities, which may eventually lead to actual candidacy for a political body. Many different factors influence this process including, on an individual level, social background, personal characteristics, demographic factors and role orientation. Further, the socio-political environment of a country will effect the recruitment process.

The process of selection determines which citizens, from the pool of those who are eligible and active in politics, are eventually seen as qualified for a representative position. The process depends on the electoral system in use. In many, it begins with selecting a list of candidates and extends to the actual nomination for a seat on a party list or selection to be a party's candidate in a specific constituency. Where the position on the list is very high or nomination is to a constituency where election is likely to be assured given past voting patterns (a safe seat), selection is tantamount to election. In the selection process the same factors are of importance as in the process of recruitment; however, other criteria are also important, including support and experience within the party. The process of selection is heavily dependent on the electoral system. In most democracies the political parties function as the selectors. The decision of who selects and by which criteria the selection is done, is however largely dependent on the political and party culture.

In some countries, the pathway to parliament has virtually been completed with the selection. The election provides the final decision on which candidates will become members of the representative bodies. In systems of proportional representation the electoral success of a party simply finalizes the matter, while in single-member district systems the election has more impact. For the election, the type of voting procedures used, such as weighted voting or preferential votes on a list, can be crucial to the electoral success of women candidates.

The electoral chances of women are analysed in terms of each of the steps in the process (see figure VI). The effect of any of the various factors will differ from country to country or, within one country, from party to party and from election to election.

Figure VI. Process of incoporation into decision-making

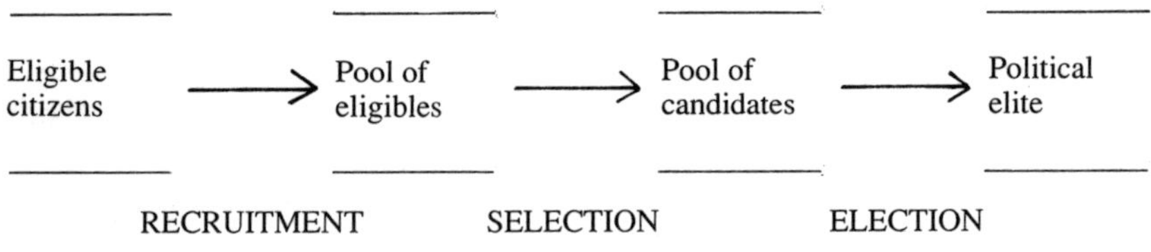

RECRUITMENT

Recruitment refers to the process whereby potential political activists are drawn out of the general population. The emphasis here is on active participation in organizations. It is the first step towards leadership. Every society and political system has its own values, rules and procedures which affect the chances for women to become involved in politics both positively and negatively. One of the obvious explanations for the underrepresentation of women is that the socio-economic environment sets limits with regard to the eligibility and selection or nomination of women for legislative offices.

Level of development

The level of development of the country, as reflected in demographic and social indicators, may limit the participation of many women. Possibilities for women are far less in countries where female illiteracy is much greater than male, generally low living standards (as measured by nutritional status and access to medical care) and, especially, high fertility rates. The extent to which women's burden is higher, through responsibility for child and dependent care, as well as daily subsistence, will make it more difficult for the average women to become engaged in political activity. However, it should be noted that the level of development is not a completely determinative factor in election to parliaments. With the exception of the Nordic countries, there are few major differences between countries by income level in terms of the average percentage of women in parliament, as shown in table 3. There is little evidence that the level of development affects voting, the most elementary form of political participation.

In the country case-studies, however, some development constraints are suggested as obstacles to women's political participation. The Algerian case-study pointed to the inherent effects of low levels of development, such as the persistent illiteracy and low educational levels for women. In the case-study on the United Republic of Tanzania the fact was noted that in the past very few women were literate and that the majority of women were involved in agricultural production (food and cash crop production), which were barriers to women's participation in politics.

Political climate

The recruitment of women for parliament depends heavily on the general political climate of the country. Authoritarian and military regimes tend to restrict open political competition, which affects women as well as men. When a country is involved in armed conflict, including wars, foreign invasion and civil strife, the political process is necessarily disrupted. Women's participation may be constrained by the physical danger implied by these situations, although it should be noted that in many cases it was the participation of women in independence struggles or resistance to aggression that became the basis for their claim to full participation in decision-making.

Social climate

More general factors in the prevailing social climate of a country can affect the number of women who achieve decision-making positions. An example is the predominant religious practice of a country. In her working paper for the Expert Group Meeting, Staudt observed that women's public voice may be forbidden or hidden in countries where religious fundamentalists rise to State power. The example was given of female students in Iranian universities who, after the 1979 revolution, were not allowed to directly question the professor, but had to write their questions and hand them to a female inspector who would then pass them to the instructor. She noted that these types of rules have 'devastating effects on women's political voice'. In general, it is reasonable to state that some religious practices encourage and strengthen de facto inequality of women in the family and in society. This may be in terms of role definition and it can be reinforced within the religion itself by denying women the same access as men to priestly functions, decision-making or adjudication of religious law. The stance of some religious authorities on birth control may have a negative impact on women's advancement.

Whether based on religious practice or cultural tradition, in many countries, whether developed or developing, strict notions exist of male and female roles in society. They are often based on biological differences in reproductive functions and are often reflected in relatively coherent, complex patterns of ideas, practices and cultural experiences which can be termed a society's 'gender ideology'. This gender ideology usually specifies that the male role is to take care of public and community affairs while the female role is the nurturing of the family. The ideology thus distinguishes between the public sphere as a territory where males dominate and the private sphere where females are assumed to have responsibility.

These stereotypes are conveyed first by the family, as part of early socialization, then by schools, later through sexual division in work and are further strengthened by the media. By reinforcing an image of women and of men in society based on well-defined attributes and social roles, the stereotypes constitute an obstacle to the full and free participation of women in political life. As the former Minister for Women's Rights in France, Yvette Roudy, expressed it:[14]

> In the minds of many citizens, a politician is always a man, and posts of responsibility and prestigious offices are still reserved for men. The familiar French expression homme politique is telling in this connection.

Attitudes differ in different countries regarding women's participation in public life. In some countries, the majority is said to believe that women should not participate in politics but rather should remain in the home. Many differences in men's and women's political activism have often been explained by gender differences in political socialization, the process by which political values and attitudes are conveyed to individuals. Women are expected to have less political ambition, less political efficacy and less interest in political affairs, which are seen as the male domain. Women who are socialized to believe this, may lack confidence in their own political capabilities. In addition, women potential candidates who believe that voters and party élites will not support them because they are women, may decide not to run because their probable prospects would be limited.

Many of the case-studies cite this gender ideology as a major barrier to women's access to political decision-making. In the Philippines, for example, the lack of women's participation was attributed to traditional attitudes or socio-cultural biases that disparaged or discouraged women's participation in the area of politics. One reason given was the long tradition in which men occupied top positions in society, because men were perceived as being stronger and more capable. Most women tended to desist voluntarily from participating too actively in politics. This attitude was particularly widespread among women in the rural areas. It was suggested,

---

[14] Council of Europe, 'Proceedings of the European Ministerial Conference on Equality between Women and Men' (Strasbourg, Council of Europe, 1986), p. 12.

however, that this attitude might change somewhat since a woman had been elected president.

In the Algerian case-study, three obstacles related to the social climate and gender ideology were discussed:

- Socio-cultural resistance, which tends to continue the roles and functions of women in the family and in society according to tradition, with tasks for women confined to domestic activities and procreation and a complete identification of social life with family life;

- Conservative social attitudes based on prejudices that deny women responsible positions based on arguments connected to 'feminine nature', which is perceived to be incompatible with politics;

- Extremist beliefs about the nature of Islam that tend to exclude women from public life.

One of the reasons that women in the United Republic of Tanzania were said not to take part in politics as frequently as men was negative social attitudes towards women as leaders based on deep-rooted and long-standing traditional practices and customs. The religious values stereotyping a woman as a mother and wife have often discouraged women's development and advancement and it was stated that many women have developed inferiority complexes because of a long history of insubordination, humiliation and suppression. Similarly, Venezuela was said to be an example of a country with a masculine-oriented culture (sometimes referred to as machismo). A consequence has been a general distrust in the ability of women to hold a leadership position.

There is, however, evidence in some countries that the gender gap in political attitudes is narrowing. For example, in the case-study on Austria it was mentioned that the traditional explanation of the underrepresentation of women in political decision-making no longer held true. Opinion surveys showed that the interest expressed by women in political issues and their interest in having female representatives in political forums had grown. Research mentioned in the Spanish case-study supported this finding. There was no confirmation that women were less interested in politics, at least at the level of verbal declarations. Women had a positive identification with such progressive values as democracy, liberty and equality and they gained an acceptable level of political information, mainly from radio and television.

The extent to which circumstances related to the general advancement, such as an increase in the participation of women in the paid labour force, or greater parity in educational access and attainment, is narrowing the gap between women and men in political attitudes, needs further study.

There are important links between the political and social climate of a country and the opportunities for women to emerge from their private domains. In many developed countries, society is organized in such a way that it is difficult for women to become involved in public affairs. In many Western industrialized countries, for example, child-care facilities are extremely scarce, and characteristics of the labour market, tax laws and regulations all reinforce traditional role patterns and inhibit women's employment. In non-industrialized countries, reducing fertility and improving education are necessary conditions for the advancement of women. Provided women have fewer children, better education and the means to compete on an equal basis with men for good employment, there is a hope that they will also begin to be more visible in politics.

There are immediate barriers that restrict the opportunities for women to enter politics. Two of the most important and comprehensive explanations of women's disadvantaged political position are the structural barriers, especially lack of resources, and societal factors such as the double burden and other domestic constraints.

Structural barriers

Explanations based upon a group's place in the social structure emphasize the importance of differential access to political resources. Many political scientists see the persistence of women's lack of political power as a predictable outcome of the ways in which advantages are distributed in society.[15] Structural barriers refer to educational level, professional experience and levels of income.

Education is one of the greatest forces for change in women's lives because it influences women's chances of obtaining paid employment, her age at marriage, her control over childbearing, her exercise of legal and political rights and her chance of acquiring political power. A higher level of formal education facilitates involvement in political party activities. For that reason, when women's educational level is lower on average than men's it reduces women's chances of holding office because it leads to a smaller pool of potential activities and therefore candidates.

A second important political resource is occupational status. Research has shown that women's participation in political life depends largely on their access to employment which gives them not only material independence, but also certain professional skills and greater self-confidence. Women often have an unfavourable situation on the labour market with regard to the skills that are considered desirable for politics. When women are in the remunerated labour force - and in many countries women have less access to jobs - they often focus their education and career development on what are often termed 'nurturing professions', which have not been considered good training for political leadership. Women are often concentrated in occupations that allow little flexibility to decide on leaves of absence and work hours, a flexibility that is very useful for political leadership.

---

[15] J. Lovenduski, Women and European Politics: 'Contemporary Feminism and Public Policy' (Brighton, Wheatsheaf Books, 1986), p. 129.

A third political resource is income. While the electoral system largely determines whether a candidate needs money to finance his or her political campaign, in countries where there is no party ticket, such as the United States, individuals have to finance their own entry into politics. Where women are financially dependent on their husbands or relatives, this may not be possible. For example, until recently in many African countries, the family finances belonged to and were managed by men. Except for family and personal expenses, women had no access to extra funds to plan and run for public office.[16]

The importance of education, occupational status and income was often mentioned in the case-studies. In the United States, relatively high educational and occupational status were major components of eligibility. These attributes are typical of members of the United States Congress. Individuals without academic training or from lower status occupations appear to have little chance of being selected to the Senate and to the House of Representatives.[17] In France as well, most men have an education that helps them in their political careers. Women have fewer years of education and are less likely to take scientific courses. However, when the educational background of French women politicians is compared with that of their male colleagues, it appears that their background is more or less the same.

The Netherlands has one of the lowest participation rates of women in waged labour in Europe, with a rate of 35 per cent compared to an average of more than 50 per cent in the other countries of the European Community (except for Ireland). Background data from Dutch women parliamentarians illustrate the importance of education and occupation for women. Women members of parliament were more likely than their male colleagues to come from families with higher status (measured by the profession of the father) and families with a history of political participation. There was, however, little difference between men and women MPs in terms of the level of education. From 1918 to 1986, half of the MPs, regardless of sex, had university degrees. Moreover, in contrast to the female adult population, the majority of women MPs actively pursued a profession before their election to parliament.

In Japan, there has been a slight increase in the political participation of women. One of the reasons given was the improved access of women to higher education. Since the mid-1950s the number of girls attending senior high school, college and university has been increasing. The more education women receive, the stronger is their sense of social participation, particularly in terms of locating job opportunities or engaging in voluntary service outside the home. More Japanese women are pursuing professional careers, a trend that has been accelerated by the enactment of

---

[16] For information on the African Countries, see Inter-Parliamentary Union, 'The Participation of Women in the Political and Parliamentary Decision-Making Process: Reports and Conclusions' (Geneva,1989), p. 38 and Kathleen Staudt and Harvey Stickman, eds., op. cit.

[17] D. Sainsbury, 'Women's Routes to National Legislatures: A Comparison of Eligibility and Nomination in the United States, Britain and Sweden' (Barcelona, European Consortium for Political Research, 1985).

the Equal Employment Opportunity Law in 1985. Prior to the enactment of the Law, girls with higher educational background experienced greater difficulties in finding a job on an equal level with men. Together with the increase in number and percentage of female college and university graduates in industry, there have been increases in managerial staff, professional and technical workers and clerical workers.

In Venezuela, the increase in educational level was one of the reasons given for why more women could be found in political bodies. For Venezuelan women, education was undoubtedly the most effective instrument for social mobility and access to decision-making levels. There has been an increase in the enrolment of women into university and high school institutions although women still tend to choose different fields than men.

In the United Republic of Tanzania, educational background, experience and certain skills are said to be an advantage for obtaining votes or being appointed to decision-making posts in government ministries and other organs. Very few women meet these requirements. Education, both general and specialized, has not been equally provided to boys and girls in the United Republic of Tanzania. Until recently, educational opportunities for women were less than one third than those for men. The reasons were embedded in Tanzanian traditional life as well as in a colonial legacy of the educational system which favoured boys over girls. Educational opportunities are now open equally to both men and women, but a consequence of past unequal provision of educational opportunities is the small number of educated women who can compete equally with men for top jobs in the country.

A study of background characteristics of women legislators in the Philippines illustrates the importance of political resources such as education and occupational status. Most women parliamentarians in the Philippines are economically well-off and highly educated. Most, if not all, come from well-known political families. In the Philippines, clearly an élite socio-economic background is a decided advantage, especially for women, for being appointed to a top position in parliament or government.

The Indian case-study, prepared by a member of parliament, illustrates the structural barriers for women to participate in politics:

> Age-old traditions, hackneyed notions about the restricted role of women and denial of adequate opportunities to them had for long prevented any real change in their status. Fortunately, the situation is no longer static. The growing role of women in public life, the impact on their lives of modern education and training, the effect of progressive social legislative efforts, their increasing participation in gainful economic activity have all set in motion forces of transformations. The emerging picture of the educated Indian woman in our urban society, is that of a person determined to participate in decision-making, both within and outside the home. But in India almost two thirds of the women live in rural areas and it is the lives of these women that truly represents the reality of Indian women. Most of them are landless women, working for a paltry wage. For those women local

leadership has to be encouraged and effective participation ensured. Only then can the quality of their lives be changed.

Situational barriers

Lack of political resources is not a sufficient explanation for women's underrepresentation in parliaments. For example, in Poland or in the Soviet Union, women have the same level of education as men and have similar occupational status. Despite this, the participation rate of women in parliament has been decreasing. In many Western industrialized countries also, women have begun to achieve the same levels of education and occupational status as men but, except for the Nordic countries, parliaments do not reflect the gender balance of the electorate.

Situational factors, the circumstances in which women find themselves, can be another barrier. Most women become wives and mothers. The age at which women marry and begin childbearing, the number of children they have, and their ability to control the time of pregnancy through contraception, all have important links to women's social status, health, economic well-being and political involvement.

In some societies, being married can be a disadvantage for women seeking to enter politics. For example, in some African societies, it is not acceptable for a woman to run for office in the area where she lives with her husband as this would imply that she rules the village of her husband, a violation of traditional roles. Marriage arrangements make it even harder for a married woman to run for office in her own place of birth as this could be perceived by her in-laws as the equivalent of declaring public divorce, as is the case when a woman has decided to go back to her people. As a result, in these African countries the participation of women in politics is limited even though they want to take part.[18] In European countries before the Second World War, it was difficult for married women to put themselves forward as candidates, as it was taken to violate norms of household headship. Moreover, party officials believed that mothers were unfit to perform in a legislative position.

Except for some of the Scandinavian countries, the political rights given to women have not been accompanied by societal adjustments that would ease the public role women have achieved the right to exercise. Due to the absence of a supportive system consisting of child-care facilities and flexible working hours, it has been extremely difficult for a mother with small children to be a politician. Mothers are often not able to control the allocation of their time, while the hours of a politician are often unpredictable. A logical consequence has been that many high-level political women simply choose to remain unmarried. Historically, professional women chose this option, and studies from various countries note a contemporary parallel. High-level political men do not have to make this choice - they marry and have children. At one extreme is a 1986 German family court case in which the

[18] Inter-Parliamentary Union, Statement by Naomi P. Nhiwatliwa, parliamentary representative of Zimbabwe, 1989, p. 38.

judge ruled that politics and childbearing were incompatible and awarded custody of the child of Green Party executive member Margarete Wolf Mayer to the child's father.[19]

There is some evidence that when mothers become politicians, they often feel a sense of guilt for not devoting themselves completely to their families, as is expected by society. In a large-scale study of women candidates for the Congress of the United States reported in 1981, Mandel discovered that the interviewees expressed a strong feeling of guilt:[20]

> There is guilt associated with not being home for adolescent children, with neglecting a husband, with exposing the family to the glare of discomfort of adjusting their own lives to the homemaker's absence. There is guilt about neglecting or assigning low priority to all the daily tasks of running a household. Even among single women there is often a kind of guilt about not keeping an attractive home or not cooking meals and entertaining guests.

The difficulty that women face in reconciling a political career with family obligations is reflected in the fact that male politicians more often than their female counterparts have small children. As a result, women often enter politics at an older age than men, after their children have grown up. However, even after the children have left home, women have been found still to be in a disadvantaged position, as noted by Lee:[21]

> The discouraging effect of children on women's desire to seek public office also greatly restricts their ability to run for office after the children left home. Because of children, women may fail to gain the experience in their twenties, thirties and early forties that their male counterparts are acquiring. When at last they are free, they may lack the political know-how and connections to effectively compete against the more experienced men. In short, most men interested in politics, get a head start and it is very difficult for women to catch up.

A factor in the family circumstances of most people is the mental and material support of the spouse. Women politicians have been found to view their husband's support as indispensable. In many cases, the husbands of women parliamentarians are interested in politics, are members of a political party or hold a political position themselves. A husband's support for his wife's political career, however, cannot be taken for granted, especially if her career competes with that of her husband or

---

[19] Women of Europe (Brussels) No. 46, 15 May/15 July 1986, p. 20.

[20] Ruth B. Mandel, 'In the Running: The New Woman Candidate' (New Haven, Ticknor and Fields, 1981), p. 91.

[21] M. M. Lee, 'Why few women hold public office: democracy and sexist rules', Political Science Quarterly, vol. 91, No. 2, pp. 297-314.

contrasts with traditional ideas about the division of labour within the family. With regard to Margaret Thatcher when she was Prime Minister of the United Kingdom, Vallance notes:[22]

> It is in any case probably not without significance that the woman who has gone further than any other in British politics, Margaret Thatcher, has a husband several years older than herself, who had come to the end of his own successful career just at the point where Mrs. Thatcher's star was in the ascendant.

The difficulties faced by female politicians resulting from their responsibilities as mothers and housewives and the absence of any adjustment by society enabling them to fulfil their tasks, is also reflected in the case-studies. The author of the case-study on Venezuela, now a senator, regards the housewife/mother occupation as one of the biggest obstacles for Venezuelan women to achieving a career. The author of the Philippines case-study, also a senator, affirms that the huge demands on the politician's time and efforts impinge on women's responsibilities towards her family.

In the case-study on the United Republic of Tanzania, the author, a long-time member of parliament, recalls that reproductive roles have tied women to housekeeping and child-care chores. As in many developing countries, the women are overworked, over-burdened, and over-concerned with family subsistence and survival, so that there is little time for them to think of competition in politics. Marital status has often worked against women who have emerged to compete for leadership positions. Some husbands have directly or indirectly discouraged their wives from seeking and competing for top leadership positions. Divorced or unmarried women have also been considered negatively and at times unfavourably whenever they have sought leadership positions, even when they were qualified for such positions.

An analysis of the background characteristics of all the female (145) and male (1,208) parliamentarians in the Netherlands in the period 1918-1986 shows that situational variables, such as being married and having children, have been important factors. The data show that sentiments about the role of married women and mothers appear to have changed, even in politics. During the first period of analysis, 1918-1946, only half of women MPs were married, and most were without children. In the final period of analysis, 1977-1986, nearly three quarters of women MPs were married, and some 40 per cent had children, although the children were usually grown up by the time their mothers reached political prominence.

Political parties, parliaments and other political bodies work according to schedules largely determined by male work patterns. They have not had to take into account that many women undertake a disproportionate share of domestic responsibilities in addition to paid work. This inevitably acts as an impediment to political participati-

---

[22] Elizabeth Vallance, 'Women in the House: A Study of Women Members of Parliament' (London, Athlone Press, 1979), p. 69.

on for many women and tends to reinforce men's predominant role in politics.

Gender equality
The extent to which gender equality is being achieved constitutes a further factor in enhancing the participation of women in politics. Countries differ in terms of whether constitutional provisions for equality have been translated into laws to promote equality between women and men or policies to ensure this equality. In countries where legal impediments to women's political participation were abolished at a very early stage, it would be expected that relatively more women are involved in politics than in other countries. It is possible to measure gender equality, not only in terms of laws, but also in terms of the extent to which women have de facto equality of access to education and employment. Many of these indicators have been published by the United Nations in The World's Women 1970-1990: Trends and Statistics.[23]

SELECTION

The process of selection determines which citizens from the pool of those recruited into political activity are deemed to be qualified for a political position and put up as candidates. It is the critical stage for women to move into leadership positions.

How selection takes place varies according to the electoral system of a country. In some countries, proportional representation is the rule, by which parties receive seats in parliament in proportion to the votes they receive. Parliamentarians are drawn off of lists of candidates put up by each party. In other countries election takes place in defined constituencies where the winner is the candidate or candidates with the largest number of votes, what are termed herein 'majority systems'.[24] It is sometimes hypothesized that women more easily achieve a greater share of political positions under a proportional representation electoral system. Under this system, political parties draw up national lists of candidates for parliament which are presented to the voters. It is the party which determines the order of their list and thereby decides the persons to be elected, although the number of seats won is dependent upon a party's share of the total valid vote. In this system, the actual competition for a parliamentary seat takes place within the party rather than on election day, since the voters decide only on the relative strength of the different parties. This means that, with the exception of the person at the head of the list,

---

[23] United Nations publication, Sales No. E.90.XVII.3.

[24] Research has been undertaken, mostly in Western industrialized countries on the relationship between the electoral system and the selection of women to run for parliament. See, for example, S. Carrol, 'Women Candidates in American Politics' (Bloomington, Indiana, Indiana University Press, 1985); R. Darcy, S. Welch and J. Clark, 'Women, Elections and Representation' (New York, Longman, 1987); and W. Rule, 'Electoral systems, contextual factors and women's opportunity for election to parliament in twenty-three democracies', Western Political Quarterly, Vol. 40, No.3, pp. 477-498.

personal electoral appeal is not the most important feature for a candidate.

There are several reasons why a system of proportional representation may be more receptive to women candidates and more favourable to their election to parliament. First, there is often a belief that men have a greater electoral appeal than women. In majority electoral systems, success is completely dependent on the selected candidate and his or her perceived attributes. In systems of proportional representation, candidates run as a team on a party slate to which women are often added as a means of broadening the party ticket to appeal to as many different kinds of elector as possible.

In contrast, the single non-transferable vote, as used in Japan, or the single-member district system of the United Kingdom, the United States and other countries which modelled their electoral systems on those two countries, tends to lead to a focus on the appeal of the individual candidate to the electorate. Women running in majority systems may be perceived to be less able, to have less experience and to lack the aggressive campaign style felt necessary to gain a majority of the votes. In that sense, they are presumed to have less appeal than men. Selection committees seek candidates who are 'fighters' with a firm base in the constituency, criteria more often found among men than among women.

The size of the district and the number of representatives per district is also a factor in majority electoral systems. Research shows a positive relationship between district size and the number of women elected. The larger the district, the more women elected. In smaller electoral districts there is a lesser turnover of representatives than in larger districts. And a low turnover has been pinpointed as a major reason for women's low representation in parliaments, since it is difficult to defeat an incumbent legislator, and most incumbents are men.

Some illustrations of the importance of the electoral system in whether women can obtain political power can be found in the case-studies. For example, in Greece, a list system was introduced in 1985. This was believed to create greater opportunity for parties to place more women in the National Assembly by running women at the top of the list. In the election that year, there was a loss of one woman member of parliament. This was considered a double loss since the implementation of the list system should have allowed women to be placed in electable positions by all the parties if those parties so decided. A headline in one daily newspaper commented: 'The great loser of the elections are women. With a list constructed by men for men.' The reinforced proportional representation system used in Greece - with the exception of the elections in 1989 when a form of simple proportional representation was used - gives large parties an advantage, and it is the large parties that have not given women favourable positions for election.

When a system based on crossing out the names of unfavoured candidates was used in Greece, this did not benefit women candidates because of the need for large sums of money to campaign and compete with male party members for seats, especially in single-member districts. A regional breakdown shows that women were elected mostly in the Athens-Piraeus region, where electoral districts were multi-member. Moreover, women were more acceptable in large urban constituencies than in smaller communities and villages.

In the United Republic of Tanzania, a majority electoral system, MPs and representatives in local government councils have to appear before the public to be seen by the voters. The case-study states that the majority of women candidates feel shy and have very little experience in political campaigns so the electoral system poses a problem for them.

Despite the presumed advantages of the proportional representation system, in Austria, for many years, the list system did not particularly favour the election of women since most of the female candidates were given lower places on the list of proposed candidates which, in turn, reduced or eliminated their chances for election. In five national elections between 1970 and 1983, only 12 per cent of the candidates were women. The author of the case-study suggested that in part this was because of what was termed 'permanence of mandates'. This was the practice of repeated re-election of current office holders, usually men, which made it almost impossible for new candidates, particularly women, to enter. For example, at the beginning of each term during the period, 80 per cent of the seats in the lower house were occupied by MPs who had held a seat in the preceding legislative period.

Selection procedures

The procedures used to nominate or endorse candidates for representative bodies can also affect the likelihood that women will be selected. In multi-party systems there are differences among parties in the practices followed. Three factors are important: who makes the selection; the selection criteria used; and whether there are any special policies to strengthen the position of women candidates.

Initial selection is either made directly by voters or as a result of internal selection within parties, depending on the system in use. For example, candidate selection in the United States is generally decided through primary elections whose function is to select candidates for the general election. Here the voters and not the parties make the final decision about candidates, and the role of the parties is limited to endorsement and sponsorship. Winning a primary depends to a large extent on first gaining the backing of supportive groups with resources. Studies of the electoral success of women candidates in primaries show that they have had little chance of winning what are termed 'open-seat' primaries (elections with no incumbent). Women have difficulty in becoming the nominee in contests when there is a reasonable chance of winning. In general, women candidates have less money to finance their campaigns and have more difficulty in developing a resource base. Support from non-governmental and voluntary organizations can be a valuable asset, but the fact that women have lower membership rates in business and professional organizations works against them, as does the fact that they are usually not part of the leadership of trade unions, which are often influential in elections. In some countries, trade unions are allowed to put up a list of affiliated candidates.

In cases where the party selects the candidates, whether this is done by the national leadership or the local or regional branches, the locus of selection is important. In the United Kingdom, for example, the local party organizations of the Labour Party are generally autonomous in selecting candidates for their districts. A committee consisting of local party members makes the selection. Whether the gender composition of these committees affects the number of women eventually selected, is unclear. Positive findings are reported for Norway, but in a study of selection committees in the United Kingdom no significant differences were reported.

In general, a decentralized selection process has tended to be more disadvantageous for the selection of women than a more centralized nomination process. National party leaders are more concerned about the male-female balance than are the local or regional branches. In contrast, decentralized procedures induce tougher competition, resulting in fewer chances for women to obtain a secure district or place on a list.[25]

Parties may also differ in selection criteria. Candidates with higher educational and occupational status are preferred but, for some parties, a long party career is an advantage. In other parties professional or community experience has more weight. The involvement of women in non-political community, school and religious organizations can work in their favour in politics since organizational support is an attractive asset for political parties looking for potential candidates, and even non-political involvement can help to develop political skills.

The most common route for women to obtain a high-level decision-making position is through previous political positions. Many parties view demonstrated political experience as the most crucial requirement for a potential candidate.

Special policies to improve the position of women in the selection process have served to ensure at least some selection. Two broad categories of these mechanisms to provide for minimum levels of female representation can be described: reserved seats and quota or target-setting. Quotas or targets are often established by political parties themselves. Under this policy a certain percentage of all candidates for a position or selection have to come from a certain group, either as a minimum or as a range within which that group should fall. The difference between quotas and targets is whether they are mandatory or indicative.

A system of reserved seats means that a certain number of seats in the parliament are earmarked for a particular group which might otherwise be unrepresented or underrepresented. Only candidates belonging to that group can compete for these

---

[25] Sainsbury, op. cit.; J. Lovenduski and P. Norris, 'Selecting women candidates: obstacles to the feminization of the House of Commons', European Journal of Political Research, vol. 17, 1989, pp. 533-562; Elizabeth Vallance, 'Women candidates in the 1983 General Election', Parliamentary Affairs, vol. 37, No. 3, (1984), pp. 301-309; R. Koole and M. H. Leijenaar, 'The Netherlands, the Predominance of Regionalism,' Candidate Selection in Perspective, M. Gallagher and M. Marsh, eds. (London, Sage, 1988), pp. 47-71; and H. Valen, 'The recruitment of parliamentary nominees in Norway', Scandinavian Political Studies, vol. 1, 1966, pp. 121-166.

seats. Usually set in constitutions or electoral laws, the system of reserved seats has already been adopted by countries such as Pakistan (20 of the 237 seats) and the United Republic of Tanzania (15 of the 244 seats in the National Assembly) and, in the past, Bangladesh (30 of the 330 seats) and Egypt (31 of the 360 seats).[26]

Egypt provides an example of the various issues surrounding the reserved seats approach. In 1979, President Sadat decreed that 30 seats for women should be added to the Egyptian parliament and 20 per cent of the seats in the local, district and provincial councils should be filled by women. In the election that year, 200 women candidates competed for the 30seats, while three women defeated men for non-reserved seats. In 1983, a first attempt was made to abolish the reserved seats. That year, the parliamentary women worked behind the scenes and convinced their male colleagues to withdraw the proposed cancellation of the reserved seats for women. In 1986, however, a revision of the electoral law which, among other things, eliminated the reserved seats for women, was passed. Women themselves were divided on the issue of abrogation. Those in favour of the system of reserved seats for women believed it was needed in order to give women assistance and encouragement in a society still bound by traditional views against women's role in public life. Those opposing the system argued that:

- The time had come for women to compete with men on an equal footing;
- The reserved-seats formula actually held women back by acting as a ceiling rather than a floor;
- Many of the 30 women MPs were said to have a 'very poor' record;
- The reserved seats were just another manifestation of tokenism, which enabled the parties to avoid dealing with the real issues facing women by putting up the requisite woman candidate and considering their duty done.

In the end, the reserved seats were abolished and the election in 1986 resulted in only 18 women MPs. In the 1987 elections, the number of women elected to the parliament declined to 14.[27]

Even though temporary affirmative action measures, such as reserved seats and quota setting, have been criticized as token gestures, experience indicates that achievement of their objective depends on the use made of them. Quotas increasingly have been considered essential in order to accelerate women's advancement in politics by encouraging women to enter politics. For example, quota setting in Scandinavian countries has been very successful. Ten political parties in the Nordic countries have introduced quotas. The Norwegian Labour Party, that country's largest, introduced quotas for internal bodies in 1981 and for the party's list for

---

[26] See Inter-Parliamentary Union, 1989, p. 9.

[27] K. Howard-Merriam, 'Guaranteed seats for political representation of women: the Egyptian example', Women and Politics, vol. 10, No. 1 (1990), pp. 17-42.

public elections in 1983. The result was that after the election in 1985, women constituted 42 per cent of the parliamentary party. In 1981, women in the left-wing People's Alliance Party in Iceland formed a coalition at a party congress and succeeded in getting almost 50 per cent women elected to the Central Committee of the party. The party then introduced quotas for women. In both cases, the women used their new strength in the internal party organization to ensure the implementation of quotas for women on the party lists. After the election in 1985 in Norway, Prime Minister Gro Harlem Brundtland, a woman, appointed a cabinet composed half of men and half of women. When the Government changed and a new coalition, headed by the Conservative Party, held office, the same number of women were appointed. In 1991, three of Norway's major political parties are headed by women.

In India, the Congress Party stipulates that 15 per cent of its candidates in state elections should be female. In France, in 1979, government legislation required that no more than 80 per cent of the candidates for local office could be of one sex. The West German Social Democratic Party established a quota of 40 per cent in 1988, and the Dutch Labour party decided in 1987 that there must be at least 25 per cent women in the parliamentary party and internal party bodies.[28]

One of the problems with quota setting is that even if it is approved formally, it may not work in practice if no sanctions are applied when the quotas are not respected. Depending on how they are set, quotas can serve to define the maximum number of women representatives rather than the minimum number. Thus, for example, with a 20 per cent quota, when 20 per cent women are nominated, this may be considered enough. Such a quota would still represent a form of discrimination, since women comprise at least half of the population. As an alternative, more countries are setting targets or quotas based on a range from 40 to 60 per cent for either sex.

Some of the case-studies comment on the selection criteria used by parties to nominate candidates in different countries. In India, for example, many women contest seats as independents, which implies that the political parties are by and large reluctant to field women as candidates. In Costa Rica, women who have been elected to the Congress were all very active politically prior to the point where they were designated within their political parties and were elected by way of the mechanisms each party has to select candidates for Congress. These women were said to have left behind many myths or stereotypes of what a family's role in society should be. They had decided to participate under the same standards as men in the fields of politics and government, and many times had been faced with

---

[28] R. Darcy, S. Welch and J. Clark, 'Women, Elections and Representation' (New York, Longman, 1987), p. 119; D. Dahlerup, 'From a small to a large minority: women in Scandinavian politics', Scandinavian Political Studies, vol. 11, No. 4, (1988), pp. 275-298; M.H. Leijenaar, 'De geschade heerlijkheid: Politiek gedrag van vrouwen en mannen in Nederland, 1918-1988' (Den Haag, SDU-uitgeverij, 1989), p. 193.

difficulties they had to overcome, namely marital problems and not having sufficient time to share with their families. An obstacle for Algerian women was that they were not particularly integrated into public life and only a few women were members of the party or involved in other mass organizations. Consequently, women were not an organized force and had no base from which to enter politics.

The case-study on Austria noted that the resulting limitation of representation to a few women did not correspond to the percentage of women in the total electorate or in the parties. It also meant in practice that the few women elected found it difficult to form the alliances necessary for effective political functioning. When elected, the same criteria for the nomination were used again to determine the division of parliamentary tasks. For example, the appointments to parliamentary committees and task forces were determined by the political parties according to party interests rather than women's political considerations. They followed the traditional gender divisions of labour in society, which meant that women were not represented sufficiently in the consideration of many issues which were very relevant to them but did not fall within traditional female categories.

In the Netherlands, to become a candidate for parliament it is thought to be highly desirable to be well-known within the party. A long party career not only brought this necessary reputation, but was also valued as a sign of strong party affiliation, indicating that the candidate would be a trustworthy representative. An empirical study of the length of membership and the number of activities carried out by women within the Dutch parties showed that they had less experience than men, which hindered their chances of being selected. Using community experience instead of party experience as a criterion for selection tended to be more advantageous for women.

In the 1989 elections in Greece, the results of women's and men's votes revealed that in districts in Athens for which statistics were available, twice as many women as men voted for women. This suggested that women had been more highly sensitized than men by the recent 35-per-cent-quota campaign popularized by the Greek women's movement.

The Swedish case-study identified a number of obstacles to women reaching equal representation:

- Unclear or secret rules for recruitment and appointment;
- Coopting practices;
- Recruitment emphasizing a military background for employees (mainly for defence issue bodies);
- Recruitment undertaken in a formalistic way;
- A small base for recruitment;
- Low visibility or secrecy in the decision-making body.

The results of an empirical study of women parliamentarians showed that women within the decision-making bodies in Sweden were often in the second level, that is, women were often deputy members and in lower positions in the hierarchy than men. Concerning recruitment, the principle of appointing by seniority also worked against the female parliamentarians. Furthermore, the interviewees stated that the persons who made the appointments often did not perceive suitable women. Another conclusion was that when persons within an authority were not directly elected by the electorate but chosen by those elected, the representation of women in many cases declined.

In the Japanese case-study an example is given of how to overcome certain barriers. For the 1987 local election, an affirmative action plan was carried out to give financial assistance to new women candidates since standing for an election was costly. The plan proved to be effective as there were many more new women candidates, of whom 90 per cent were successful. As a result there was a 50-percent increase in the number of women legislators at the local level.

Party ideology

The political ideologies professed by political parties sometimes affect their attitudes towards participation by women. For example, liberal political thought emphasizes equal opportunity in a competitive political market, while socialist and communist ideology contain special commitments to female emancipation. More traditional conservative ideology may emphasize female participation in the family rather than politics. In practice, parties with a centre-to-left ideological orientation have had relatively higher female representation than other parties, as has been pointed out in a study by the Council of Europe. In countries where larger numbers of women now sit in parliament, parties of the left were the first to elect women. Subsequently, other parties also began to elect women even though ideologies did not specifically emphasize women's participation. This difference between the left and the other political parties has existed for some time. In Italy, for example, 16 per cent of the Communist Party's representatives in the Chamber of Deputies were women as early as 1948, compared with 6 per cent for the Christian Democratic Party.[29]

Similarly a study of women and politics in Latin America and the Caribbean shows that at the beginning of the century, liberal parties not affiliated with religious groups, radical parties and the non-religious democratic right in general supported women's struggle to obtain citizenship. Since that time there have been many women visible in the parties on the left although few have held leadership positions.[30]

Political parties founded on specific religious aims do not strongly emphasize women's integration in the party, partly because of their emphasis on the applicati-

[29] Council of Europe, 'The situation of women in the political process in Europe,' Women in the Political World in Europe, part II (Strasbourg, 1984), p. 87.

[30] United Nations, Economic Commission for Latin America and the Caribbean, 'Women and Politics in Latin America and the Caribbean' , ECLAC Serie Mujer y Desarrollo No. 3 (Santiago, 1989) (LC/L.515), p. 18; see also J. Jacquette, ed., 'The Women's Movement in Latin America: Feminism and the Transition to Democracy' (Winchester, Unwin Hyman, 1989).

on of religious principles to public policy relating to the role of women in the family, abortion and sexual behaviour.

A recent European phenomenon is a tendency for smaller, left parties (especially the ecological or 'green' parties) to have a greater number of women in their parliamentary party than the larger liberal parties. One explanation is that the membership of these parties consists of rather young, well-educated people who have considerable free time and commitment. Women in these parties seem to be willing to stand for election and party membership supports this. A second reason may be that these parties challenge not only the established economic and social order, but also the traditional division of tasks and roles between women and men. Many of these parties have established the practice of including women as half of their candidates to show their willingness to break with traditional gender ideology.

The Austrian case-study made two assertions which are relevant in this context. First, that the Social Democratic Party had always appointed a higher proportion of women than the more conservative parties. Secondly, it was a time when traditional political patterns were being questioned and issues considered that demanded an approach that cut across established party lines. It was noted that in the formation of new political groups around issues such as peace, ecology and social justice, new gender and age structures were likely to be found and more women, older and younger people were being represented in these groups. This new political climate was beginning to encourage established political parties to respond as well.

In the Netherlands, the religious parties had traditionally criticized women's participation in the public sphere more than the other large parties. At the beginning of this century, these parties opposed women's suffrage on the grounds that politics should be considered a man's job. Voting privileges were granted to women not so much because of a change in attitude, but more because the majority in parliament feared a possible revolution of the left-wing as had occurred in Germany, and since women were thought to be more conservative in their voting behaviour, the participation of women in politics would be a stabilizing factor. The conviction that women were more likely to vote for the religious parties was also one of the reasons why the parties with a religious base in the Second Chamber supported, with a few exceptions, the change in the Constitution which granted women the right to vote. The Netherlands case-study suggested that the negative attitude of the religious parties, which have a major importance in Dutch politics, towards the political participation of women was an important explanation for the low number of women in parliament.

Political culture

What may be termed the 'political culture' of a country, the values, attitudes and behaviours relating to politics, can be important factors in women's participation. The case-studies contain many examples of this.

The Indian case-study stated that the formal political structures are hierarchical and vertical, along the lines that society itself is structured. Women, however, need to be community oriented and relate to each other for effective participation. The formal system, as it exists was established as a reflection of male values with very little input by or with the consent of women. It was definitely not structured to reflect women working together. In India, this conviction has led to the birth of many women's organizations and groups outside the formal political structure.

The French case-study asserts that politics is considered a man's game. French women do not like some of the rules of the game, including the club atmosphere, the idea that it is necessary to dominate others, to have to repeat oneself continuously, and the seemingly interminable meetings.

The Austrian case-study notes that de facto decision-making, which takes place in informal unofficial groups, reduced the formal decision-making process to a function of ratifying decisions already taken by acclamation. These informal groups were almost exclusively male and their lack of transparency effectively prevented any change of the situation. There was a double effect of gender discrimination by which the lack of female decision makers at the highest levels perpetuates the lack of women at subordinate levels and continued their situation of limited bargaining power. The parallel lack of access of women to informal channels of communication and decision-making reinforced this trend. This was reflected not only in political appointments in the parties and in the Government, but also in the civil service hierarchy and in the bodies representing organized economic interests, such as the trade unions, employers associations and chambers of commerce and of labour.

Women's organizations within political parties

The existence of women's organizations within political parties also has an effect on participation. Usually only party members are allowed to participate in the nomination process as selectors or candidates. Consequently, the more women who are party members, the more women are likely to be candidates. Many political parties have a special division or organization for women party members. Research has shown a positive relationship between the strength and organizational structure of women's organizations within political parties and the number of women candidates.

Women's organizations can help to lower the entry barriers for women by providing a training ground for new recruits. They can also provide post-election support to women who have been elected, by providing a political base as well as a network of other women from which support and advice can be drawn.

Women's organizations can also be considered as a pool from which recruitment can take place. Leadership positions in the women's wing of a political party may lead to a representative post in the parliamentary party. In addition, women politicians whose backgrounds include involvement in women's organizations are likely to be more committed to ensuring that the political system is made accessible to other women. An illustrative example is the previously mentioned efforts of women in the party executives in Iceland and Norway, who used their position in power to ensure that the party would adopt quotas.

In a study by the Inter-Parliamentary Union, several countries reported the existence of women's sections within parties. In Cameroon, the single political party has a women's wing, which is entirely run by women. In Canada, the three major political parties have each established organizations within their party structure to encourage women to stand as candidates. These groups are designed to train women in the skills necessary to raise money, plot strategies and run campaigns. In Gabon, the Women's Union of the Democratic Party of Gabon aims in particular at educating and promoting women in all fields to enable them to participate actively. In Rwanda, within the National Revolutionary Development Movement, there exists a woman's organization; and in Zimbabwe, the ruling party, the ZANU-PF, has a woman's wing with representation at the national level. Each of the five parties in Japan with a seat in both houses of the parliament has a woman's bureau. In Mexico, the ruling party, the Institutional Revolutionary Party, has established a national council for the participation of women; and in the Republic of Korea, the ruling Democratic Justice Party, the Reunification Democratic Party and the New Korea Democratic Party all have women's affairs divisions.[31]

The Kaum Ibu (later Wanita UMNO) is the women's organization of the United Malay National Organization (UMNO), the principal political party in Malaysia. The Kaum Ibu strengthened the women's party choice, provided a social outlet for women, including sewing and cooking classes, served as a women's forum to discuss politics and established a safe arena in which to run their affairs. For the party, the women's wing mobilized many voters, provided a communication network from officials through women leaders to women, brought a steady income, and strengthened the party base. One can say that such a place is necessary for women as a first step to becoming involved in politics.[32]

One negative effect of having separate women's organizations is that women may not be integrated into the party structure and may receive only token positions on party executive committees. In that case, women can be easily considered as a special interest group rather than a large mainstream constituency within a party. In a study of 2,000 members of the political élite in Mexico, 2 per cent of them female, none of the 40 women used the women's organization in the party on their route to leadership positions.[33] In Colombia, however, most of the 41women party

---

[31] Inter-Parliamentary Union, 'Participation of Women in Political Life and in the Decision-making Process: A World Survey as at 1 April 1988', op. cit., pp. 36-37.

[32] V. H. Dancz, 'Women and Party Politics in Peninsular Malaysia', (New York, Oxford University Press, 1987) and W. Karim, 'Malay women's movements: leadership and processes of change', International Social Science Journal, 1983, pp. 719-731.

[33] Roderic Camp, Mexican Political Biographies is cited in an unpublished paper by Kathleen Staudt as is Carlota Aguilar, 'Women and class agendas among activists in Northern Mexico'.

activists studied credited the women's branch for giving them a start in formal politics.[34] Nevertheless, their career paths within the party were short and the men who controlled the party accorded them only token positions. In both cases the numbers of women were too small for them to use gender as a basis for political leverage.

The case-study of India mentions the important roles played by the women's organizations in the parties. The increase in the number of women voters and active participation by women in voting motivated almost all the political parties to pay special attention to organizing women, campaigning among them and choosing them to contest elections. In previous decades, campaigning among women and soliciting their votes had been undertaken rather casually. By 1989, parties had regular forums, cells and front organizations specially for women. These cells not only mobilized and campaigned among women, seeking their support for the parties' positions during and between elections, but also took up women's issues themselves. They organized rallies and demonstrations on women's issues, passed resolutions and lobbied the Government in favour of specific policies.

Another difficulty is that women's organizations have to work within the framework of the broad interests of the party and often do not take an independent stand on women's issues. Political parties are concerned lest their women's groups should emerge as self-reliant entities, independent of party control, and they therefore monitor those groups closely. In some cases, this has caused women's groups to renounce the parties and form autonomous groups of their own.

While it was not formally the women's organization of a party in Greece, the Union of Greek Women (EGE) was closely associated with one party. Its relationship to the political party ranged from being a satellite interest group to a fairly autonomous organization for the mobilization of women. That party was able to mobilize women to a certain extent through the women's organization and at the same time to maintain control over them. However, during 1988/89 the Greek women's movement became more militant and transformed itself into a more independent interest group. Many in the women's movement were disillusioned with the policies of government and political parties on women's issues, and so they formed a Women's Coordinating Committee (WCC) consisting of 18 women's organizations and 8 women's sections of parties. They demanded a quota of 35 per cent participation of women in all the organs of the parties and in all decision-making posts in government and in parliament. Despite a strong electoral campaign by WCC in favour of the 35 per cent quota, which was in the end not granted, the June 1989 elections proved once again unfavourable for women.

Influence of international norms for the advancement of women

International standards regarding political participation of women can also influence

[34] S. Harkness, 'Colombian women in party politics', Research on the Interweave of Social Roles: Women and Men, vol. 1, 1980.

the degree to which parties are willing to nominate women. Women's groups can cite these standards as part of their effort to pressure Governments to undertake affirmative action programmes aimed at getting more women involved in politics. Examples of this are found in the case-studies.

The Austrian case-study suggested that political will to increase the representation of women can be created by pressure on the Government as the result of international obligations under conventions, such as the Convention on the Elimination of All Forms of Discrimination against Women, as well as from the electorate. The case-study of the United Republic of Tanzania stated that the attitudes of men and women had been changing rapidly since 1975, especially following the 1985 Nairobi Conference. There had been extensive discussions, conferences and workshops on women's issues.

The case-study on Japan noted that the women's movement was first stirred by International Women's Year (1975) and had been increasing in political, educational, legal and economic fields or in family life and civic movements all over the country. These movements and changes had been supported intellectually and technically by the global movements of international friendship, by the United Nations Decade for Women, by the world conferences on women and their resolutions, and by the Nairobi Forward-looking Strategies. The ratification of the Convention on the Elimination of All Forms of Discrimination against Women had been effective in helping to remove the last legal barrier between the sexes in employment in 1985.

ELECTION

Election constitutes the final step on the pathway to politics. Many of the factors involved in the process of recruitment and selection influence women's chances to be elected. Of particular concern is whether they combine to make women less electable than men.

One indication is found in the results of three surveys carried out in the countries of the European Community. The responses to the question: 'In general do you have more confidence in a male or female politician, representing your interests in parliament?' are shown in table7.

Table 7. Perceived competence in male or female politicians, in countries of the European Community, 1975-1983
(Percentage)

Sex	Year	More confidence in a man	More confidence in a women	No difference	No response
Men	1975	42	6	46	6
	1977	47	6	42	5
	1983	34	4	60	2
Women	1975	33	11	50	6
	1977	33	16	44	7
	1983	27	9	61	3
Total	1975	38	8	48	6
	1977	40	11	43	6
	1983	30	6	61	3

Source: Femmes et hommes de l'Europe en 1983, Bruxelles, 1984, p. 121.

In 1983, more than half of both the male (60 per cent) and female respondents (61 per cent) answered that they had as much confidence in a female as in a male parliamentarian. This represented a growing perception that gender made no difference. Women more frequently than men showed expressed confidence in a female but when one sex was preferred, it was overwhelmingly the male, even among women. Part of the basis for these perceptions may be the fact that the professional experiences of women candidates are generally different from what is suggested by the electorate as necessary credentials for politicians. As was stated by Carroll in 1985 on the basis of research:[35]

> Like their male counterparts, women candidates are drawn largely from professional and managerial occupations. However, a pattern of sex differences in occupational background exists. The concentration of women candidates in traditionally

[35] S. Carroll, 'Women Candidates in American Politics' (Bloomington, Indiana, Indiana University Press, 1985), p. 26.

female fields, such as teaching, social work and nursing, may work to their disadvantage. To the extent that voters believe that certain types of professional credentials (e.g. law) equip one for office holding, while other types (e.g. teaching) do not, many candidates may be perceived as lacking the necessary occupational backgrounds for office holding, despite their professional status.

Electoral appeal is also defined by other characteristics. Mandel describes at great length the difficulties women candidates campaigning for a seat in the United States had with notions about the 'right image'.[36] While male candidates had image problems as well, related to their appearance and demeanour, they had a greater scope for a variety of images because there was less doubt about men's basic suitability and competence as politicians. There were many examples of successful male politicians, but the voters lacked a clear image of a successful female politician. The Mandel study suggested that the desirable image for political women included many contradictory characteristics: 'not too young, not too old, not too voluptuous, not too prissy, not too soft-spoken, not shrill, not too ambitious, not too retiring, not too independent, not too complaining about being excluded, not too smart and not too uninformed'. Women who have succeeded in politics and who occupy strategic positions are still judged in terms of female attributes. Often, their clothes and appearance are singled out for comment.

The type of election seems to have an impact on the chances of women candidates. In many countries more women participate at the local and regional levels than at the national level. It is often asserted that local politics is more attractive to women than are other political positions since concern at that level is with issues important to women, such as housing, roads and traffic, schools, childcare, welfare and support for women's activities. Direct contact with citizens occurs more often and, most important, local government is often not a full-time job and can be practised near home.

Local governments often serve as recruitment pools for parliament and other national political decision-making positions. The participation of women in local politics therefore can be an indication of the probability of future representation of women in national legislative bodies.

There is some evidence that women are more likely to obtain a political position by appointment than when the system is based on direct election. One explanation is that the authorities who make the appointments are often more concerned with a balance between the relevant social groupings, including women, than the mass electorate.

Family ties

Family ties influence chances for election. In countries where name recognition by voters is an important factor in elections, family relations can provide this for women. It has been noted that many women who are elected to office are wives,

---

[36] Mandel, op. cit.

widows, sisters or daughters of politically prominent men. It may be that they are perceived as providing continuity with the politics of the man. In majority systems with single member districts, such as the United Kingdom and the United States, many of the first women members of parliament succeeded their husbands in the seats. In Ireland as well, until recently, the seat of a deceased husband, father, uncle or other close relative was a main channel for aspiring women candidates: 'If the localist function, with all the ready-made contacts established, could continue with but a change in face, then a woman was as acceptable as a male relative.'[37]

Voting procedures

Voting procedures themselves may work to the advantage of women wanting to serve in public office, if women use them. In some political systems preferential voting based on either weighting votes for individual candidates on party lists or voting across party lines can be used to indicate a preference for women candidates on the lists. An example was Norway in 1971. Voting procedures in force until that year permitted voters to change the order of the names of the candidates by striking out names. For local elections in 1971, Norwegian women's groups made a concerted effort to elect women by explaining to the voters how to make use of preferential voting and at the same time appealing to them not to remove the names of women candidates from the lists. This resulted in a large increase in the percentage of women councillors in many cities in Norway. For example, in Trondheim it increased from 20 to 54 per cent, in Asker from 26 to 57 per cent and in Oslo from 28 to 56 per cent.[38]

Preferential voting can be advantageous to women candidates because it enables them to appeal to women voters. Since in most countries women form a larger voting bloc than men, the women's vote can be used as a means of putting pressure on parties to nominate more women.

The case-study of Austria shows how the outcome of an election can determine the number of women parliamentarians. When a party makes unexpected gains in an election and therefore has more positions available than it had expected, it is more likely that a higher proportion of women will be appointed, apparently because not all positions have already been promised to men by informal distribution before the election.

In the case-study of Japan an example is given of the power that can be exercised by women voting as a bloc. In the 1990 elections to the Tokyo Metropolitan Assembly and the national House of Councillors, the number of women representatives increased from 9 to 17 and in the upper house elections, from 10 to 22.

---

[37] F. Gardiner, 'Role of deputy, political culture and implications for women's access to parliament.', paper presented at the joint session of the European Political Science Association; Bochum, Federal Republic of Germany, 2 - 6 April 1990.

[38] S. Sinkonen, 'Women in local politics', E. Haavio-Manilla, Unfinished Democracy: Women in Nordic Politics, (Oxford, Pergamon Press, 1985) pp. 81-105 and I.N. Means, 'Women in local politics', Canadian Journal of Political Science, vol. 5, No. 3 (1981), pp. 365-388.

Women constituted a larger part of the electorate, by 3 per cent, than men. Three political issues were said to have caused this increase. First, Japanese voters, especially women, were angered by bribery charges made against several politicians. Secondly, the party in power passed a bill, without public consent, that levied a 3 per cent tax on items related to daily needs, such as bread and milk, that particularly angered the housewives who had to pay it. Thirdly, the leader of the party in power was found to have purchased sexual favours from a geisha. This scandal helped to make the Prime Minister and his party unpopular among women voters.

Politics had previously been perceived as a man's world. During the election, politics was presented as analogous to house-keeping on a national level, dealing with matters of daily life. It was stated that women candidates had greater knowledge of this aspect of life than men, and were better able to make life more pleasant and safe. As a result, more women than before stood for election and the governing Liberal Democratic Party lost its majority in the House of Councillors for the first time since the party's founding in 1955.

The case-study of India states that recently more women have become increasingly politicized, which has been expressed in the way they cast their votes. It is accepted that Indian women will not vote blindly, or as their male relatives order them to. Recent elections have shown that women can exercise their vote independently, pointing to the decisive role of women in the electoral outcome.

In Greece, the age-old system of patronage prevails, according to the case-study. Personal relationships at all levels of power play an important role in securing employment in general, and in high-level appointments in particular. It is said that most of the 13 women elected in 1981 to the parliament were either well known before the elections or had made a reputation for themselves through their husbands or fathers. In a study of the 13 women members of Parliament it was stated that most came from families of political importance, with a more or less stable clientele.

CHAPTER III
WOMEN IN GOVERNMENTAL DECISION-MAKING

The effect of women on political decision-making cannot be assessed by merely quantifying their representation in elected assemblies. It is also necessary to consider their participation in both the political executive and the higher ranks of the civil service. The political executive, which provides leadership for the State and the political system, is drawn from the ranks of those in power at the time. The modern political executive exists in many forms with its authority variously vested in a person or in a collective. However, it is most commonly centred on a president or a prime minister and works through a cabinet of ministers with specific responsibilities or portfolios. The way in which members of the cabinet are selected and the amount of power exercised by ministers differ widely from country to country. The number of women who have come to lead the political executive as president or prime minister and the career path they followed to get there will be discussed below.

Women's presence at the highest levels of formal governmental decision-making is a recent phenomenon in most countries and their numbers continue to be few at the ministerial level. Moreover, not all ministers are of equal importance and, again, it is necessary to look beyond the statistics of women's participation to the relative significance of the portfolios they hold.

The other component of the government executive is the permanent salaried civil service, which normally remains in office to carry out the policies of whichever politicians happen to be in authority. Positions in the senior ranks of these public bureaucracies offer opportunities of wielding considerable influence and power in decision-making. Moreover, participation of women in the civil service is also significant for another reason: as the largest employer in many countries, the public sector offers women employment and experience. Governments and women themselves can use this as an instrument and opportunity for the empowerment of women, not only in politics, but in the workforce and society as a whole. Public bureaucracies can play an extremely important part in implementing equal opportunity laws and pioneering affirmative action programmes, child-care arrangements and campaigns against sexual harassment that may serve as examples to other sectors of the labour market.

WOMEN AT THE TOP: PRESIDENTS AND PRIME MINISTERS

Quantitative analysis of women in the highest decision-making positions is easy. In world history, up to 1991, there have only been 18 women who have been elected as head of State or Government of independent countries. These are shown in table 8. That this is a recent phenomenon is shown by the fact that in 1991 all but two of these women (Golda Meir and Indira Ghandi) were still alive. Moreover, in May 1991, 8 were still in office, the largest number in history. This means that only some 5 per cent of the world's countries were led by women. Those who have reached this level of power can be compared on the basis of their biographies. The section is drawn from an analysis made by Kathleen Staudt for the Expert Group Meeting based on a review of biographies of the women who had become elected heads of State or Government.

Table 8. Women elected heads of State or Government in history

Individual	Country
Presidents	*Country*
Corazón Aquino*	Philippines
Violeta Chamorro*	Nicaragua
Vigdis Finnbogadóttir*	Iceland
Lidia Geiler	Bolivia
Ertha Pascal-Trouillot	Haiti
Isabel Perón	Argentina
Mary Robinson*	Ireland
Prime Ministers	
Siramovo Bandaranaike	Sri Lanka
Benazir Bhutto	Pakistan
Gro Harlem Brundtland*	Norway
Eugenia Charles*	Dominica
Edith Cresson*	France
Indira Ghandi	India
Golda Meir	Israel
Maria de Lourdes Pintasilgo	Portugal
Milka Planinc	Yugoslavia
Margaret Thatcher	United Kingdom
Khaleda Zia*	Bangladesh

*Still in office as at 1 September 1991.

Women have thus reached the top political leadership in countries in all regions except Africa and Eastern Europe. About half of them have entered politics by way of their family connections. Corazón Aquino of the Philippines, Siramavo Bandaranaike of Sri Lanka, Violeta Chamorro of Nicaragua, Isabel Perón of Argentina and Khaleda Zia of Bangladesh took up political leadership upon the death of their husband. Indira Ghandi of India and Benazir Bhutto of Pakistan were daughters of previous prime ministers.

Others of the 18 rose through the ranks of political parties. Gro Harlem Brundtland, Eugenia Charles, Edith Cresson, Golda Meir and Margaret Thatcher all served in a variety of party and cabinet positions before becoming prime minister. Lidia Geiler and Maria de Lourdes Pintasilgo reached power during turbulent periods of political change in their countries and had been involved in politics for a considerable time.

Most female political leaders have had a college or university education. Vigdis Finnbogadóttir was a teacher. Charles was a lawyer and Thatcher trained as a chemist and subsequently studied law, having spent some time in scientific research prior to entering politics. Aquino, Bhutto and Chamorro studied in the United States.

Although the women who have headed their countries came from a variety of backgrounds, their experiences suggest that family connections and long involvement in a political party are important factors in attaining such high positions. The issue of family connection, which is not unknown among men who reach high position, is perhaps the major obvious gender difference in the background of women top leaders. In a situation where women's political resources are limited, the assets provided by symbolic succession as well as the political skills learned in the family political environment may have been necessary for those women to reach power.

WOMEN IN MINISTERIAL AND SENIOR-LEVEL DECISION-MAKING

The low percentage of women at the very top of government is matched by a low percentage of women in the next levels of governmental decision-making. On average only 4.2 per cent of those in the influential positions considered in the average country were women. While it was obvious to most observers that the presence of women at this level was rare, there had been no systematic examination of the phenomenon prior to 1989. As part of the preparations for the Expert Group Meeting on women and decision-making, the Division for the Advancement of Women undertook to examine the incidence of women in these decision-making positions.

To obtain the necessary information, data from the World-wide Government

Directory of 1987-88[39] were used to establish the relative participation of women and men in high government office around the world. The Directory, which covers national or federal Governments, but does not include state, provincial or lower levels of administration, includes information supplied by 155 countries in 1987. While most gave information on various levels, 14 of the countries only included positions at the ministerial level or above. Others gave a broader coverage, and some listings included a wide range of public enterprises and advisory boards.

In order to ensure comparability, the inventory of office-holders was limited to those whose ministerial or government position entailed responsibility for making and executing policy. This included all those who held formal portfolios for specific ministries as well as other decision makers who would be in cabinet discussions by virtue of their functions (e.g.security advisers and the leaders of central banks). However, the heads of advisory boards, public enterprises and the armed forces (apart from those included in defence ministries) were excluded. For most countries, the government listing was usually limited to officers with policy or executive responsibilities, but for several countries with large and complex governmental structures it was necessary to enlist the help of knowledgeable informants in order to determine which positions should be included.

The entries in the directory were classified according to the sex of the occupant, its relative level and the type of government ministry involved. Within each ministry or government department, four levels of office were considered. These varied from country to country, according to administrative practice, and selection was generally based on job titles, although these were not necessarily always clear indications of position in hierarchies (as in the case of presidential assistants in the United States, for example). However, the rough divisions were the top level consisting of prime ministers, presidents and ministers, as well as other highly influential positions, such as heads of central banks, and three senior but sub-ministerial levels: deputy or assistant ministers and their equivalents; secretaries of state and permanent heads of government departments and their equivalents; and deputy directors of ministries and their equivalents.

The ministries themselves were classified into six categories: the office of the chief of state, the office of the prime minister (if applicable), political ministries, economic ministries, ministries concerned with law and justice, and social ministries. The political group was comprised of those often called the 'flag ministries': foreign affairs, defence and internal or home affairs. Finance, industry, agriculture and trade ministries, and the central bank made up the economic group. Law and justice included justice ministries, the court system and institutions such as ombudsmen. The social classification included those that deal with education, health, culture, social welfare, community development, youth, women's affairs and similar responsibilities. In some cases a ministry's activities fell into two classifications and

---

[39] National Standards Association, World-wide Government Directory of 1987-88 (Bethesda, Maryland, 1987).

it was necessary to assign it to a category on the basis of its apparent primary function.

In the majority of countries, women were completely absent from ministerial levels of decision-making and in a third (51 countries in total), there were no women at any of the senior (sub-ministerial) levels (see table 9).

Table 9. Countries in which there are no women at ministerial or senior level, 1987

Region	Ministerial level (%)	All senior levels (%)	Number of countries
Africa	60.8	41.2	51
Asia and the Pacific	79.5	46.2	39
Latin America and the Caribbean	69.7	24.2	33
Eastern Europe	33.3	0.0	9
Western industrialized	26.1	17.4	23
All	60.0	32.9	155

The greatest progress at the ministerial level has been achieved in developed countries, most of which have at least one minister. Most developing countries do not yet include women in their cabinets. At the other senior levels, most countries have at least a few women, although there are regional variations here as well. Only in the nine countries of Eastern Europe were there women at senior levels of decision-making.

However, for most countries, when women were present at decision-making levels, the proportions were low. The percentage of women at all senior levels by region is shown in table 10.

Table 10. Average percentage of women in decision-making levels, 1987

Region	Level				
	Ministerial	Vice-ministerial	Department director	Department deputy director	All
Africa	2.7	5.1	4.7	4.9	3.6
Asia and the Pacific	1.6	2.2	3.1	4.2	2.0
Latin America and the Caribbean	2.7	6.8	13.8	10.0	6.0
Eastern Europe	4.5	2.4	2.7	1.6	3.7
Western industrialized	9.0	12.3	5.5	9.2	6.8
All	3.5	5.7	5.9	6.3	4.2

When all levels are seen together, it is clear that over 95 per cent of government decision makers are men. Although the differences between regions is not great, since the levels of women's participation are low overall, the most pronounced disparities lie between Asia and the Pacific and in Eastern Europe.

These regional variations can also be seen when the different levels of decision-making are examined separately. The situation is worse at the ministerial level, but it does not improve greatly at lower levels. In general, the proportion of women increases as the decision-making level is lower, a pattern found in Asia and the Pacific and, to a lesser extent, in Africa. Conversely, in the Eastern European countries before restructuring, it is almost the opposite: the higher the level, the higher the percentage of women, a phenomenon probably caused by the token appointment of women at the ministerial level while the posts at the lower levels were filled by regular (and not political) career mechanisms reflecting a bias against women in career advancement.

There are variations within regions in terms of government decision-making, just as there were variations in terms of women in parliament. Using a subregional classification used by the Statistical Office of the United Nations, some of these differences can be seen in table 11 and figure VII.

Table 11. Average percentage of women in ministerial and other senior level decision-making positions, 1987.

Region	Average percentage
Africa	3.6
North	1.1
West	5.4
Central	3.3
East	3.2
South	1.9
Asia and the Pacific	2.0
Southwest	1.4
South	3.4
Southeast	1.0
East	0.8
Oceania	4.0
Latin America and the Caribbean	6.0
Central	5.0
Caribbean	10.1
Tropical south	2.9
Temperate south	1.6
Eastern Europe	3.7
Western Industrialized	6.8
Northern Europe	12.4
Western Europe	5.4
Southern Europe	5.4
North America	8.9

Figure VII. Percentage of women decisionmakers at different levels, 1987

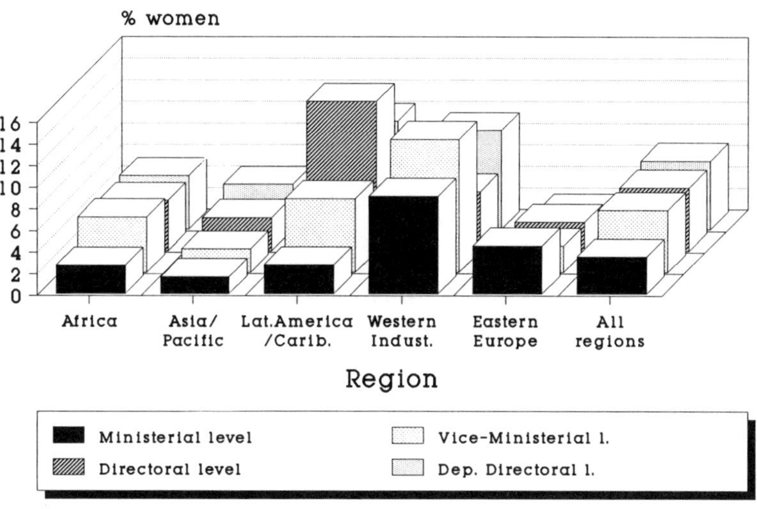

Subregions with particularly low representation of women in senior level decision-making include North Africa and Southwest, South-East and East Asia. Only two subregions have a relatively high (over 10 per cent) representation of women: these are the Caribbean countries and Northern Europe, which includes the Nordic countries. However, it should be noted that even in those regions, the proportion of women at senior levels of decision-making is inferior to their representation in parliament.

The subregional breakdown demonstrates that a higher proportion of women in decision-making does not automatically follow from economic development. Countries of West Africa, Central America and Western and Southern Europe have the same average percentage of women at these levels. The average for developed countries taken as a whole is higher than that for developing countries taken as a whole, but if the Nordic countries were not included the differences would narrow. Among the developing countries, the major oil-exporting countries and the major exporters of manufactures - who constitute what the World Bank terms the middle-income developing countries - have lower average percentages of women in decision-making (0.9 per cent) than any other sub-group, except the Asian centrally planned economies (0.8 per cent).

The women who hold decision-making positions tend to be concentrated in ministries that deal with issues that are often defined as women's concerns; they seldom occur in ministries that are considered more powerful. The average percentage of women found in different types of ministry are shown in table 12.

Table 12. Average percentage of women in different types of ministry, 1987

Region	Office of the head of state	Office of the prime minister	Ministries: Political	Economic	Law and justice	Social	All
Africa	1.1	2.6	1.6	1.6	3.4	8.6	3.6
Asia and the Pacific	1.5	0.5	0.9	2.0	0.7	3.3	2.0
Latin America and the Caribbean	1.0	11.0	6.3	2.8	9.6	10.9	6.0
Eastern Europe	7.1	4.2	2.1	3.2	3.1	9.0	3.7
Western industrialized	7.7	12.8	5.1	3.6	4.0	13.8	6.8
All	2.3	5.7	3.0	2.3	4.0	8.6	4.2

While women are found in all types of ministry, they are more prevalent in social ministries or in prime ministers' offices. This latter may reflect the fact that many ministers of women's affairs are without portfolio and are administratively located in the prime minister's office. The lowest incidence of women occurs in economic ministries and offices of heads of State. The patterns in the various areas are similar to the overall average, with some exceptions. In countries in Latin America and the Caribbean and in Western industrialized countries, there are relatively more women in the office of the prime minister, probably reflecting the tendency to locate women's affairs in that area. Women in Latin America and the Caribbean are relatively better represented in law and justice ministries, probably reflecting the fact that they have had access to the legal profession longer than in other regions.

The distribution for ministerial rank decision makers is presented below by type of ministry. However, some examples can be drawn from a comparison of the different sub-ministerial levels. The general pattern shows a slightly higher proportion of women at lower senior levels than in the higher ranks. For example, in Latin America, women make up, on average, almost onethird of decision makers in social ministries at the level of department director or deputy director. However, they also make up almost 20 per cent of the department directors and on average, one third of the deputy directors in political ministries reflecting the entry of women into the higher civil service. In the Western industrialized countries, however, the average percentage of women is higher, for all types of ministry, at the ministerial or vice-ministerial level than at the lower levels of department director or deputy director. This may reflect the lower civil service career prospects of women there compared to political routes to decision-making.

WOMEN CABINET MINISTERS

Women cabinet ministers (see table 9) are, on average, almost as scarce as women heads of State or Government. In 1987, there were no women at that rank in 93 countries. The average proportion of women at ministerial level was 3.5 per cent.

The incidence of women as cabinet ministers, like the presence of female parliamentarians, varies according to the political system of the country. Women are more likely to be represented in cabinets drawn directly from parliament than in those appointed in presidential systems. They are less likely to appear in military Governments or regimes ruling without a parliament. However, even this does not give the true picture since fully half of the countries that enlist their cabinet or political executive from the elected members of parliament had no women among them at the time of the study. In presidential systems, the chief executive has the power to select ministers from a wider pool using criteria beyond membership in parliament as a basis for appointment. Despite this, 59 per cent of the countries with these types of cabinet had no women ministers. In 1987, 81 per cent of the countries under military rule and 90 per cent of those with non-military regimes but no parliament had no women at the ministerial level of decision-making. In part, this reflects the fact that women are not usually among the leadership of military establishments, although there have been exceptions, for example, when the military Government was the result of a revolution in which women participated as combatants. Examples include Nicaragua after the Sandinista revolution and Zimbabwe.

Table 13. Average percentage of women ministers in different types of ministry, 1987

Region	Office of the head of state	Office of the prime minister	Ministries: Political	Economic	Law and justice	Social	Total
Africa	1.2	0.7	1.0	0.9	2.1	7.4	2.7
Asia and the Pacific	4.8	0.0	0.0	1.6	0.0	3.2	1.6
Latin America and the Caribbean	0.0	6.3	3.2	0.5	3.6	8.4	2.7
Eastern Europe	0.0	0.0	2.2	4.3	14.3	4.8	4.5
Western industrialized	12.5	9.4	9.4	5.1	10.9	14.5	9.0
Total	2.4	2.7	2.7	1.8	4.0	7.5	3.5

Once in the cabinet, women are frequently assigned to the social ministries. This can be seen from table 13, which shows the average proportion of women among ministers with different portfolios. There are several possible reasons for this. Women are relatively well represented in education and the social service professions. There is a larger pool of women experienced in the management of politics in those fields. In that sense, they may be appointed to posts on the basis of their expertise. They may have demonstrated more interest in these areas than men and have expressed this concern politically. But there are also widely held assumptions about gender-based division of roles, which suggests that these areas are the most appropriate ones for women to manage in government.

It may also be a matter of the power in the post. Many of the social ministries are relatively weak; where they were strong because of the resources controlled by them, for example, in Eastern Europe prior to recent changes, women were less well represented than, for instance, in law and justice. The ministries that manage finances and the economy have few women, in any region; the same is true of the 'flag ministries'.

The career paths of those women who have reached the cabinet are very similar to those of women legislators in general. The case-studies give some indication of the process, as well as the situation of women at that level in the various countries.

The first woman to hold a ministerial level appointment in Costa Rica served as Minister of Education from 1958 to 1959. There have since been five other women ministers who held portfolios of culture, education, justice and labour. The earlier tendency to assign them to fields traditionally associated with women, such as education, or to ministries regarded as less significant in the country's economic development, seems to be decreasing. The women were appointed to the political executive by the President, and their expertise in the particular field and their prior political experience had been important factors in their selection. Their formal education, professional experience and personal ideologies had enabled them to escape many of the conventional myths or stereotypes that so often limit a woman's role in society.[40]

Although the first women parliamentary secretaries or deputy ministers in the United Republic of Tanzania were chosen in 1965, only a year after Tanganyika and Zanzibar joined to form the United Republic of Tanzania, no woman appeared in its cabinet until 1980, when 2 of the 21 ministers (9.5 per cent) appointed were women. By 1985, there were five women ministers who made up 24 per cent of the total. In 1989, there were still five women, comprising 20 per cent of the cabinet. Within the components of the union, the first women ministers were appointed to the Zanzibar cabinet in 1983. They represented 12.5 per cent of the 16 members, but by 1988 there was only 1 female minister among the 13 members.

India is one of the few countries to have been led by a woman for a considerable length of time. However, in 1989 there was only one woman cabinet minister and six ministers of state. This was the highest number in history. Since 1962, when there were two cabinet ministers and two ministers of state, the number of women ministers had varied between three and five. Although most of the women who have become ministers either in the central or provincial (state) governments have been assigned to social portfolios, others have been entrusted with the responsibility for labour, housing and energy.

Japan had three women holding cabinet posts by 1989. One was appointed Minister for Health and Welfare in 1960 and the other two became the Director-General of the Science and Technology Agency and of the Environment Agency in 1962 and 1985, respectively. However, the situation is better at the level of parliamentary vice-minister where the first woman was appointed in 1948. Since then 24 women have been vice-ministers for a number of departments including Foreign Affairs, and Health and Welfare. In 1989, the vice-minister in charge of the Okinawa Island Development Agency was a woman.

The first woman was appointed to the Austrian Cabinet - as Federal Minister for Social Affairs - in 1966. Of the seven female ministers between then and 1989, five

---

[40] 'Women in Decision-making : Case Study on Costa Rica' (United Nations publication, Sales No. E.91.IV.5).

belonged to the Socialist Party and two to the Peoples' Party. Between 1970 and 1979, there was one woman State Secretary, a post with the rank of Minister of State, in every cabinet. In 1979, the Federal Chancellor appointed an additional four female State Secretaries and at that time 6 of the 22 cabinet members were women. In 1989, there were three women, including the Secretary of State responsible for women's affairs. The case-study noted that when women have become cabinet ministers in Austria, they have frequently been appointed to newly created ministries, which means that they had to establish both the necessary political alliances in the cabinet and the bureaucratic apparatus of the newly formed department. In several cases, as soon as this was done, the ministry was given to a man in the next legislative period.

In the Netherlands, the Catholic Party appointed the first female minister in 1956. Since then, there have been 9 women in the 13 cabinets formed up to 1990. The percentage of female participation has ranged between 6.3 and 14.3 per cent. In the cabinet which came into power in 1989, the percentage has risen to 21 per cent. It was also the Catholic Party which appointed the first female junior minister, in 1953, who stayed in office, in two cabinets, till 1956. The second woman to be appointed at this level did not appear for another 15 years, in 1971. Between 1953 and 1990, only 18 women served as junior ministers in the 21 cabinets.

Examining the backgrounds of these women shows that eight of the nine who became cabinet ministers had university degrees in subjects ranging from chemistry and classical languages to law, education and economics. Seven of them had married and six had one or more children. However, their average age on entering the cabinet was about 50, by which time their children had grown up. All of them had served in several other political functions as local or provincial councillors or members of parliament, before they became cabinet ministers. The same holds generally true for the junior ministers; 13 of the 18 had university degrees. Most of them had married and had children and their average age on appointment was 47. With only a single exception, all had had previous political experience and positions. The number of ministers and vice-ministers recruited from within parliament rather than from outside has risen since the Second World War, suggesting the importance of a parliamentary career as a path to decision-making.

There has been little change in the gender composition of the Government of Greece over the past 30 years or so. The high government posts that are the seats of power have been traditionally almost the exclusive preserve of men. While the democratic governments in office before 1981 all had a female Deputy Minister or Under-Secretary for the traditionally 'woman's ministry' of Health and Social Services, the head of the Ministry was always a man. After 1981, a woman who was already an internationally famous personality became Minister of Culture and the Education Ministry was led by a woman as well. Female cabinet participation increased from 2 to 6 per cent in the 1980s, but had dropped back to 2 per cent in the interim Government of 1989. Most of the time, there was only one woman (though there were two between 1985 and 1989) among the 35members of the Council of Ministers, the body that decides on all important policy matters.

In 1966, 2 of the 17 members of Sweden's cabinet were women. By 1977, there were 20 ministers, 5 of whom were women. The figures were the same for 1987. With only one exception, the women were ministers without portfolio or in charge of labour, housing or social issues. The exception came in 1976 when a woman was made Minister for Foreign Affairs. In 1987, the five female consultative ministers had special responsibility for equal opportunities, immigration, energy, environmental issues and international aid. In 1988, the Government was made up of 21 cabinet ministers, 7 of whom were women. Since 1966 female representation at the ministerial level grew from 12 to 33 per cent. This has been paralleled by higher representation in the Office of the Prime Minister, the Ministry for Foreign Affairs and the Ministry for Defence during the same 20-year period.

However, more women have been appointed as consultative ministers, rather than as cabinet ministers with full responsibility for a department. Of the 118 cabinet ministers between 1969 and 1986, 25 (21 per cent) were women. But of the 81 full ministers, only 8 (10 per cent), were women, all after 1976. However, there were female consultative ministers throughout the two decades to 1986; 17 (55 per cent) of the 33 ministers in this category were women.

Since 1981 there have been an average of six or seven women in every cabinet in France. In 1989, there were six women who covered foreign affairs, European affairs, communications, consumption, family matters and women's affairs. This was in itself a departure from the earlier practice of assigning women to portfolios that might be generally classified as social. One of these women became Prime Minister in 1991.

In 1989, there were two women in the federal cabinet of the United States, with eight women also named to head government agencies and commissions. The first woman member of the cabinet was appointed in 1933 and served through 1945. Most subsequent cabinets had at least one woman, usually in the portfolios of labour, education or housing. However, a woman was the equivalent of a minister of trade in 1989.

Women in the civil service

The civil service provides a career path which women may use to participate in the centres of power and decision-making. Indeed, it has been suggested that their access to this level could have far-reaching effects: the expectation is that women in public bureaucracies will be aware of themselves as agents of change, and will be advocates and practitioners of management styles that place a high priority on participatory, non-hierarchical interaction between managers and employers. As more women enter the top ranks of the bureaucracy, characteristics particular to women should change not only the bureaucracy itself, but also the policy outcomes of its functioning.

Unfortunately, all over the world, women interested in public administration as a career have to overcome all kinds of barriers. Many of these barriers are of course similar to those mentioned in the previous chapter. Women's access to education is determined by their country's stage of economic development and the circumstances of their everyday life. Less education may diminish their chances of employment. The general social and political ambience is a decisive factor in their chances of involvement in public life. Women may be taught or socialized to believe that they should not aspire to careers because their proper place is at home with their children. Those who try to combine motherhood and work outside the house are hampered by the lack of support facilities. As well as these general obstacles, there may be other constraints inherent in the structures and practices of public administrations. Sex role stereotyping and gender discrimination may affect women's entry into the civil service and combine with limited access to on-the-job training to hinder their upward mobility within an organization.

The enormous variety of public service structures and systems makes it difficult to draw comparisons between countries and to define the common impediments to the advancement of women in the civil service in less general terms. As yet there is little research available on the specific problems encountered by women working in public bureaucracies. This section therefore relies on the information provided by the case-studies and data from WISTAT, which enable some detailed examination of the situation of women in high-level government and civil service positions, and an overview of the similarities and differences between the 16 countries for which the case-studies were commissioned.

There are also other reasons to consider women's presence in public bureaucracies carefully. Women are relatively well represented in the public sector in many countries, a fact which gives considerable scope for the Government to use its own policies and practices as examples to improve female employment in general.

Unfortunately, there are as yet few comparative data or research on women in the civil service, and less on their advancement through it. A survey of the position of women in the public sector of the labour market in the 16 countries covered in the case-studies suggests some general similarities that may characterize the situation of women in public administration. It should be noted, however, that the case-studies themselves vary considerably in the amount and type of information they provide. Some emphasized the role of women in the legislature and political executive, while others devoted more attention to women in the civil service, a difference that often reflects the existence or accessibility of data on women in government in different countries.

In 1988, the case-study on Venezuela noted, women comprised about a third of the formal workforce. The State was the largest single employer of female labour and 46.4 per cent of government employees were women. Although this included six women who headed departments of finance, social development, agriculture, labour, science and technology, and women and the family, promotion to the highest ranks of the civil service was usually restricted to men. Women often worked in important professional positions, but tended to start at a low level and few were promoted to positions of power and responsibility. In 1978, there were only 29,025 women, about 13.3 per cent of the total, in managerial positions in the public service in Venezuela. By 1988, the figures showed only slight improvement, with 40,520 women in these positions making up 16.4 per cent of the total. The case-study affirmed that there was little doubt that the figures reflect discrimination rather than lack of ability. Most men were hostile to the idea of a woman as their chief, and when the only union for women disappeared, women lost their advocate for a fixed share of employment opportunities. A major obstacle to their progress was the lack of support to enable them to balance their maternal and professional responsibilities. However, women's determination to overcome the difficulties they face in both public and private enterprises and the support of government bodies that encourage the development of women and the family suggest that they may do better in the future.

In 1966, there were only 90,500 women in paid employment in Algeria. The number had increased to 138,000 by 1977, and in 1987 it reached 425,000 or 10 per cent of the workforce. Most of the women were employed in education, health or general administration and 87 per cent of them worked in the public sector. However, the majority of women preferred to work in the home because of demographic pressures and the lack of child-care facilities.

The position of women in the Algerian labour market has improved as their educational levels have risen. In 1977, most women were in unskilled jobs but by 1987, 80 per cent of the female workforce had at least elementary schooling and 13.2 per cent had a university education. Compulsory education for children from 6 to 16 has had very positive effects, especially for females. In 1965/66, only 32.3 per cent of Algerian girls went to school, compared to 57.5 per cent of the boys. By 1987, the figures had risen to 73 per cent and 89 per cent respectively, and the differences in the educational levels of the sexes were very slowly narrowing. In 1978/79 the 13,000 females at the university made up about a quarter of the student body. In 1989, about 40 per cent of the country's 200,000 students were women.

These and other general improvements in the position of women have had a beneficial impact on female participation in decision-making. Although lower educational levels and persistent traditional stereotypes on male and female roles in society continued to hinder the advancement of women, the statistics indicate much progress has been made. By 1985, there were 20,000 women in responsible positions, and the number had risen to 26,300, or 17.6 per cent of the total of 149,000, by 1987. Most of these women had a university degree, professional expertise and experience in decision-making. In 1989, 357 women held high office in the public bureaucracy, including 1 inspector-general, 8 directors and 44 deputy directors in the central administration. Eight women held responsible positions in the Cour de Comptes, an important financial institution, and there were also 293 female magistrates and 2 female university rectors.

In the United Republic of Tanzania in 1989, 56.9 per cent of all public service positions were held by women. However, they were mainly doing traditionally female jobs such as teaching, nursing and typing; 80 per cent of the typists and 69 per cent of the nurses were women, but only 11.3 per cent of the managers, 6.7 per cent of the executive managers and 4.4 per cent of those in high positions were women. The first woman to head a government department was appointed to the Ministry of Community Development, Culture, Youth and Sport in 1985. There was still only one woman among the principal secretaries in 1989, although another had been made an assistant principal secretary in 1988. Two women were appointed ambassadors in 1985, making up 9 per cent of the total of 28.

Thanks to expanded educational opportunities at the secondary and university level, more women are qualifying for high positions in the United Republic of Tanzanian teaching institutions, the judiciary, the army, the police force and the medical services, and are emerging in top positions in these branches of the civil service. However, though a number now hold lower level management jobs in state agencies, national corporations and the central banks, no woman has yet been appointed to head any of these institutions. The first woman judge was appointed in 1975. She later, in 1980, became Minister of Justice and Attorney General. At the time of the study, there was one woman judge and three female resident magistrates in active service.

Traditional gender ideology is a major obstacle to women's access to leadership positions. However, another important factor is the lack of support systems and facilities to cater for those who have both family and professional responsibilities. On top of this, women have still to make up for former inequalities in educational opportunity. The case-study states that to get to the top, women often have to be more qualified than their male counterparts. It therefore takes them more time to gain the extra experience they need to be accepted. The records show that those women who have reached high-level government jobs have had to work harder and make greater sacrifices than their male colleagues in order to be appreciated and maintain their positions. It will remain difficult for women to participate in high level decision-making in the United Republic of Tanzania although paradoxically it is essential that they do so if the circumstances that now constrain them are to change.

Most of the women in India's public sector are also employed in stereotyped jobs as receptionists, typists and secretaries, nurses and schoolteachers. In 1989 it was estimated that only 4,548 (just under 10 per cent of the total) were in the top ranks of the civil service. Women constituted 994 of the 16,987 officers in the armed services (5.8 per cent) and 21 (9 per cent) of the police officers. However there were some positive signs. Indian government policies to increase the number of women in the civil service included media campaigns, training incentives and, for example, regulations to enable married employees who both work in the public sector to be posted together. The compulsory inclusion of at least one woman on every government recruitment board and the establishment of a separate register of women at all employment exchanges to ensure every list put forward for recruitment included at least 30 per cent female candidates, if they were available, provided grounds for some optimism about the possibilities for more women to enter and rise in the ranks of the civil service in future.

Although increasing numbers of women were studying law, most of them did not go on to pursue a legal career even though there was an urgent need for more female lawyers as massive social legislation and greater literacy and awareness of their rights was encouraging many more women to seek justice through the courts. The presence of women judges could be very important in assuring women's access, especially in those regions where the status of women was particularly low. More women have been appointed to the High Courts, but there was still no female judge in the Supreme Court in 1989.

The Indian case-study states that other facets of women's political participation involved safeguarding and promoting their professional interests, improving their working conditions and, above all, their liberation from oppressive power relations. These called for a collective approach in which professional groups, trade unions and rural organizations have a pivotal part to play. Unfortunately women's participation in the trade unions was far from satisfactory. Although the nature of the work they did and the way the unions functioned were partly responsible, the strong patriarchal attitudes prevalent among workers and union leaders were a major deterrent. By 1984, women made up 75 per cent of the memberships of the unions but they remained poorly represented at decision-making levels and issues of particular significance to them had not been taken up, thanks to the hostile attitudes of their male colleagues and the union leadership. Although the impact of the women's movement had made the three main unions pay some attention to women's issues by the end of the 1980s, the temporary status of most female workers, their retrenchment problems, even the wage disparities between men and women and the lack of such amenities as maternity benefits and crèches had not received the empathy and support they needed from the unions. They were simply not seen as important issues in terms of union activity.

Basic justice, equality of opportunity and support systems were needed to ensure that Indian women could participate as they should in their country's decision-making processes. This entailed a new determination and a new approach to devising appropriate measures to educate public opinion and direct popular aspirations towards the eradication of prejudices and practices based on the concept of female inferiority.

In 1975, 12 occupational categories in the civil service were still barred to women in Japan. It was not until 1988 that the doors of the bureaucracy opened fully to them and they could apply for any available position. In 1986, 34,285 women worked in the national government administration, where they made up 14.5 per cent of the staff. The vast majority of them (91 per cent) held low-level clerical jobs. The situation was different in the higher ranks: the seven women who worked as directors of bureaux or equivalent made up only 4per cent of the total of this level. Fourteen departmental heads (1per cent) and 32 sectoral chiefs (6 per cent) were women. Nor was the situation much better on any of the country's 237 advisory boards. In 1975, the 133 women on them made up only 2.4 per cent of the membership, though the number had risen to 297 (6.6 per cent) by 1988.

Women's access to important positions has been most conspicuous in the legal sphere where the number of women lawyers and judges has doubled since 1977. There were only 58 women judges or assistant judges then, making up 2.1 per cent of the total, but by 1988 the percentage was 4.1 per cent. Unfortunately the number of female prosecutors had remained fairly static: in 1988, only 32 of the 2,118 prosecutors (1.5per cent) were women.

The Government has recognized that their lower educational levels and a social climate permeated with traditional perceptions of gender roles are major obstacles to Japanese women. A body for the Planning and Promotion of Policies related to Women was set up in 1975. Chaired by the Prime Minister, its membership included vice-ministers from the departments and agencies that have jurisdiction over women's issues. In 1977 it formulated a national plan of action for the advancement of women in decision-making bodies. This required all ministries and government agencies to appoint women to advisory councils, with a target of 10 per cent female membership. It sought to encourage women on government-sponsored committees and to stimulate the employment and progress of women in the civil service and to maximize the development of their abilities. Local government bodies and institutions and private enterprises were asked to cooperate by appointing and promoting women to higher decision-making posts. However, the figures showed that although these policies had been in place since 1977, the results by the end of the 1980s were minimal. There had been some progress, but women's participation in decision-making remained very low.

Considerable information on the situation of women in the Philippine civil service was presented in the case-study, whose author was Chairperson of the Civil Service Committee of the Philippine Senate. In the Philippines, women have been more active in executive rather than the political bodies. In 1987, a survey of 500,000 government employees at all levels showed that 51 per cent of all positions, but only 18.8 per cent (29) of the 154 top positions in 18 departments were held by women. These high policy-making positions in the executive were all filled by presidential appointment, with the top posts subject to confirmation by the Congressional Commission on Appointments. The situation was better in posts such as bureau directors and regional directors, which were usually held by career officers. In 1989, 85 (27 per cent) of the 316 directors were women. Unfortunately, the incidence of women as chairpersons, presidents and board members of official financial institutions and government owned or controlled corporations was much lower. They held only 12 (9 per cent) of the 133 top positions. Although there were numerically many women in high government positions, their representation was still disproportionate in relative terms, and there was much room for improvement, even in those departments where most of the technical or professional personnel was female.

It is necessary to analyse these aggregate figures in order to determine whether old sexist divisions of responsibility prevailed. The figures support the observations that they did. Some departments were traditionally masculine. Only 12.5 per cent of the staff of the Department of Transportation, 3.1 per cent of Public Works, 11.7 per cent of Agriculture and 3.1 per cent of Environment were women. Conversely, there were some traditionally female departments: 92 per cent of the higher jobs in Social Welfare, 66.6 per cent in Tourism and 40.7 per cent in Budget and Management were occupied by women. The Education Department might appear to be dominated by women, as more than 80 per cent of schoolteachers are women, but they held only 24 per cent of the top policy-making jobs. While the dominance of women in Social Welfare, for instance, could be attributed to common perceptions of appropriate female roles and the concept that women should carry primary responsibility for family care, it was more difficult to justify the unbalanced allocation of power in the Education Department or the Judiciary.

In 1989, only 174 (11 per cent) of the 1,565 members of the judiciary were women. Three of the 15 Supreme Court judges and 6 (13 per cent) of those in the Courts of Appeal were women, although this was an improvement on the overall participation rate of 8 per cent in 1979. These unimpressive figures stemmed from the fact that the legal profession was a traditionally male sphere. In 1975, only 7 per cent of those admitted to the bar were women. The higher figures in the 1980s - 22 per cent in 1983 and 30 per cent in 1989 - signalled a significant development in the entry of women into this male-dominated profession.

In 1984, a survey of 175 senior officials, 88 women and 87 men, found that most of the women came from urban areas and high-income families and had tertiary qualifications. It also showed that they had gone through a longer 'apprenticeship' than men before reaching the senior levels. Clearly, an élite socio-economic background is a decided advantage, particularly for women, when it comes to securing high government positions. Although there were some exceptions, most of the women and men had spent considerable years in government service before they reached the top by similar paths. However, women often had to overcome traditional cultural bias in order to enter the bureaucracy. Although their recruitment was a clear recognition of their competence, their capacities were not necessarily fully developed and their careers may have been impeded by persistent constraints. In spite of the continuing increase of women in the ranks of government decision makers, their uneven distribution could be traced to conservative inertia that had its roots in colonialism as well as to male bias and to the attitudes of the women themselves. However, there were indications that women were beginning to enter non-traditional fields, and this, combined with supportive legislation and policies and their own concerted efforts, should result in significant progress in the future.

According to the case-study on the Union of Soviet Socialist Republics, more than 65 million women were employed in the industrial, administrative and agricultural sectors (most of which could at the time be considered part of the public sector) in 1980. They constituted approximately half the workforce. Sixty per cent of professionals and workers with higher or specialized secondary education were women: they made up 60 per cent of the engineers, 45 per cent of the agronomists, animal specialists and veterinary workers, over 70 per cent of teachers and doctors, 87 per cent of the economists and accountants, and 40 per cent of all scientific workers. Thirteen per cent of those who had a doctorate in science and 28 per cent of those with another higher degree in science were women.

A large proportion of the female workforce was employed in education, health, social security, retail trading, public catering and the supply, procurement and sale of materials and equipment. Over half a million of them held managerial positions in enterprises or institutions and about a million others headed their departments, sections, workshops or organizational subgroups. In 1989, 35 per cent of the members of the All Union Central Trade Union Council were women, as were 43 per cent of the central committees of the industrial branch unions. All in all, more than 9.6 million women were engaged in responsible work at the head of union committees in enterprises, institutions and on collective farms.

Despite the major socio-economic changes in the Soviet Union at the end of the 1980s which could contribute to the extension of women's role in decision-making at the local, regional, republic and union-wide level, in 1989 only 12 per cent of the managers of industrial production combines and independent enterprises and 14 per cent of all floor supervisors and their deputies were women. No information was provided in the case-study on the prevalence of women in the formal Government.

In Poland, in 1989, an increase in the number of women with university education and those who were professionally active had been accompanied by better representation in different levels of the administration. This progress had not been uniform, however. While more appeared in the lower echelons, their presence in high posts in central authorities was little more than symbolic. At the time of the study there was only a single woman minister and two female under-secretaries. However, in contrast to the general trend in Eastern Europe, their numbers were higher in the ranks of the directors, and especially of the deputy directors, of departments and they were even higher among the heads of divisions or specialist groups: 29 (5.4 per cent) of the 533 departmental heads, 76 (14 per cent) of deputy directors, 628 (27.5 per cent) of the 2,284 chief specialists and 220 (40 per cent) of the 550 in care of divisions were women. Though their numbers were gradually increasing, women in top management were still rare in Poland at the end of the 1980s, and while more highly qualified women were reaching higher positions, they were seldom at the top or in the most powerful structures.

It has sometimes been suggested that because in Poland women tend to concentrate on studies in certain fields, they do not have the qualifications necessary to reach higher positions. The facts do not support this contention as their placement between 32.4 and 67.8 per cent of the managerial positions in such feminized areas as the judiciary, health services and education showed. Although women were almost equal in terms of university education and women outnumbered men in the group with secondary education, their representation in top positions was low.

In 1983 a study showed that only 12 per cent of those who made decisions at the local level, such as chairmen of the Peasants Party, mayors and their deputies, heads of communes and directors of major departments, were women. Most of these local leaders came from peasant backgrounds. The men often had fathers who had been in the militia. The successful men and women had begun their working careers in different ways. The women usually began as office workers, teachers or technicians. The men often began as teachers or workers, but not office workers or technicians, and they were more likely to have gone straight into lower-level management jobs. In general, the women worked in less influential institutions or organizations and they were more likely to be deputies rather than chiefs. They were virtually never heads of divisions or regional offices. In 1983, a national survey found that 30 per cent of the women complained of impediments to promotion. Lack of appropriate qualifications had held almost half of them back. A quarter of them reported that their professional experience was considered inadequate. Eleven per cent were concerned that the amount of time they had to spend on household work prevented them from improving their qualifications. Gender discrimination was mentioned by 9.5 per cent.

The case-study on the United States noted that nearly 63 per cent of career civil servants in 1988 were women. In addition to the women in the national cabinet, 8 others had come to head government agencies or commissions and 97 women had been put in top government positions by presidential appointment. On the whole, however, only 10.3 per cent of the career civil servants in the Senior Executive Service, the top level of the career service, were women. And, while 27.7 per cent of career Foreign Service staff were women, only 5.6 per cent of those at the senior levels were women. However there is evidence of change. The percentage of women in professional occupations in the civil service rose from 21.2 per cent in 1978 to 29.2 per cent in 1988, and the proportion in administrative occupations rose from 22.6 per cent in 1978 to 37.8 per cent in 1988. The case-study noted that the policy of the federal Government was to provide equal opportunity in employment for all persons, to prohibit discrimination in employment because of race, colour, religion, sex, national origin, age or handicap, and to promote the full realization of equal employment opportunity by a continuing affirmative programme in each government agency.

In Austria, the question of equality in political participation and decision-making touched on a number of issues. It is necessary to consider not only women in the legislature and senior ranks of government, but also in those institutions such as the trade unions and employers' associations which represented the organized economic interests in the country's social and economic partnership and wield considerable influence on the negotiations and regulations that affect various aspects of life in the country.

A study carried out in 1980 revealed that despite their formal equality, female civil servants were mainly clustered at the lower levels of the hierarchy, just as they were in private enterprises. As a result of these findings, a Programme for the Promotion of Women has been developed in cooperation with women in different government departments. The Programme, which was adopted in 1981, set out a series of clearly defined policies on the hiring, training and promotion of women. In addition, plans of action geared to specific requirements were worked out with female liaison officers in the individual departments. It was hoped that the Plan would not only further the advancement of women in the civil service, but would also set an example to the private sector.

By the end of the 1980s, the scheme had been very successful at the middle levels of the public service, but considerably less so in placing women in the positions that have the greatest political influence. Only 2 of the 80 departmental heads were women. On the next level, 2 out of 97 divisions were run by women. Fifty-nine (8 per cent) of the 722 section heads were women, an improvement on the 1980 figure of 5.2 per cent. A higher percentage of women had managerial responsibilities at lower levels.

The composition of the power structures in the bodies that made up the Social Partnership was much the same: the percentage of women at the top was still negligible, although a woman had recently assumed the leadership of one of the major unions. The female membership of the Austrian Trade Union Federation stood at 30.8 per cent in 1986.

Women have never made up a large part of the formal workforce in the Netherlands. At the beginning of the twentieth century, only 22.5 per cent of the labour force was female. Female participation began to rise rapidly only after 1960. The proportion of married women in employment rose from 7 to 33 per cent over the following 20 years. However, in 1960, women usually left the workforce when they married. By 1979, the pattern was to wait until they were expecting their first child. In that year, 75 per cent of married women under 35 who had no children were employed, compared to only 16 per cent of those who had young children.

Women hold 7 per cent of managerial and executive positions. Their situation differs little in the private or the public sector. In 1988, there were 41,000 women in the civil service, making up 24.6 per cent of the total, an increase of 6 per cent since 1976. However, the number of women in different areas varies widely. For example they make up 16.5 per cent in the Department of Transport and 39 per cent in the Education Department. In six ministries over 30 per cent of the managers are women, but in five, which includes the traditional male preserves of finance, agriculture, transport and defence, the average representation is less than 24.6 per cent.

Very few women reach the higher echelons. Those who are in administrative or managerial positions are still a long way from the top, as the disparities between their salaries and those of their male colleagues show. In the Dutch civil service there are six salary scales, which relate to various functions. Income level I is at the bottom and level VI is at the top. The remuneration of almost 75 per cent of all female government employees, but of only 39.8 per cent of the men, is in the two lowest categories, a discrepancy that can only be partly explained by the fact that the women are, on average, younger than the men. Within each age group, women still receive less than their male colleagues.

The increase in women's employment in the public sector has not only been small, it has been happening at a rate of less than 1 per cent per annum, in spite of policies designed in 1976 to remedy this. Recruitment advertisements, for example, carry the slogan: 'The central Government would like to employ more women, and they are especially invited to apply.' Despite the good intentions reflected in this and a number of other policies and measures, there has not been much upward mobility for the women who have joined the civil service. To some extent this is said to be an aspect of behaviour patterns based on the gender roles prevailing in society generally: more than half the women who leave the civil service do so because they are pregnant. The woman who wants to pursue a career in public administration still has to choose between a profession and children. Lack of support facilities and the negative attitudes of personnel offices fearful of exceptions are both big barriers on any upward career path. In spite of the generally affirmative political climate, which encourages the recruitment of women, their situation within the bureaucracy will not improve as long as departments are unwilling to accommodate their need for more flexible hours and the provision of child care.

Female labour-force participation in Greece differs from that in other European countries in that although the percentage of women in the service sector recently doubled from 22 to 44 per cent in 15 years, in 1986 this figure was still far below the average of 71 per cent in the service sector in Europe as a whole. Nearly 16 per cent of the Greek women who were occupied in the service sector were permanently employed in banks and the civil service.

In the 27 years from 1956 to 1983, the proportion of women in the public administration more than doubled, rising from 15.7 to 38.4 per cent. Typically, much of this employment was in the traditional jobs of nursing and teaching where 59 and 51 per cent, respectively, of the workers were women. Their access to these professions had not been matched at higher levels of the administration. Until 1981, the number of women directors or deputy directors was negligible: there were never more than one or two, except in 1974 when there were four. During the 1980s, however, their representation in the ranks of the directors tripled from 5 to 15 per cent. More women also appeared among supervisors, where their number doubled from 15 per cent in 1972 to 31 per cent in 1983.

The large difference between the proportion of women at the levels of supervisor and director may be attributed to the fact that up to the level of supervisor, promotion was automatic and based on years of employment. Promotion to directorships, however, was not automatic but depended on vacancies for which the candidates always outnumbered the positions available. The competition was intense and the men tended to win. In 1975 the promotion system was changed so that the most senior applicants had to be favourably considered when a directorship became available, a modification which benefited women who could not be so easily overlooked on the basis of seniority. There has been a steady improvement in the figures since then. However, some ministries, such as justice and agriculture, remain dominated by men. Sadly, and most significantly, the personnel committees that are responsible for promotions had no women on them at the time of the case-study.

Although the figures for female employment were higher in the banking system, where 45 per cent of the staff were women in 1989, there were scarcely any in the upper ranks. Forty per cent of the personnel of the National Bank, the country's major institution, were women. Nine per cent of its men and only 1 per cent of its women were at the top level.

Sweden's target of a minimum of 40 per cent of all posts to the less represented gender has already been mentioned. In July 1986, 58 per cent of the 3,150 ministry officials were women, but in some responsible positions the figure was a less encouraging 30 per cent, and at the top it was even lower at 10 per cent. In other words, though women predominated at the lower levels, men still had the power at the top. The picture was much the same in the central government authorities. In 1986, only five (6 per cent) of these 82 bodies were led by a woman. There were six female chairpersons (11 per cent). Female participation was highest at the lowest level: 38 (34 per cent of the total) of the deputy representatives of the officials were women.

Sixteen government authorities dealt with issues relating to defence and foreign affairs. The 1970s and 1980s saw a slow but positive general trend towards greater female involvement in their decision-making. In half of these authorities this occurred at the board level and, in general, once women had been included on a board for any length of time, the authority tried to continue to have one or two women. However, if the number of board members decreased, the number of women tended to drop disproportionately.

The case-study on Spain emphasized women in the top positions in the ministries. In 1988, there were 23 female directors-general and three government delegates/civil governors. The Department of Social Affairs and the Office of the Government Spokesperson had a higher than average proportion of women in top-level posts (33 and 45 per cent, respectively); both were headed by a woman minister. Representation was particularly low in the ministries of Culture (7.7 per cent), General Affairs (6.7 per cent), Economics and Finance (4 per cent), Housing (5.9 per cent) and Agriculture and Fisheries (4.8 per cent). The ministries of Justice, Transport and Tourism, Foreign Affairs, Health and Defence had no women at all in the top positions. In fact, although the average overall representation of women at high levels had increased from 6 per cent in 1985 to 9.8 per cent in 1988, it had actually fallen in such ministries as Culture and Economics and Finance.

According to the case-study on France, in 1989 more than one third (38 per cent) of the French presidential cabinet were women, two of whom dealt with economic affairs (and one of whom became the prime minister in 1991). This is higher than the average figure overall of 24 per cent in the ministries at the senior level and suggests more definite progress had been achieved in appointed posts than in those that were filled by career civil servants.

SIMILARITIES AND DIFFERENCES BETWEEN COUNTRIES

Despite the wide range of data presented in the case-studies, it is nevertheless possible to draw some general conclusions on the representation and situation of women working in the public sector, the impediments to their career advancement and the attempts of their Governments to help them to overcome these barriers.

An important similarity is the preponderance of women in the civil service in many countries, such as the United Republic of Tanzania (56 per cent). In others, such as Japan, where it was only 20 per cent at the time of the study, the percentage was rising. Despite this, women constitute a disproportionately low number of the top-level decision makers in public administrations everywhere. Among the countries studied, only India, the Philippines, Poland and the Soviet Union had more than one or two women in ministerial positions in 1989, and it was by no means clear that these levels would be maintained even in those countries as their political situations altered.

Occupational segregation is a feature of most public administrations. In almost every country, most of the women on the government payroll were teachers, nurses or clerical employees. There was a similar dichotomy between the various areas of government: some departments, such as education, social welfare and health, were much more likely to employ women than others, such as transport, defence or economic affairs and finance. Some of the case-studies point out that the feminized departments were less powerful than the others.

These conclusions are similar to those found in a 1983 study of women in public administration in six countries.[41] That study identified six impediments to women interested in a civil service career, including socialization that instilled and reinforced attitudes that stifled rather than stimulated their aspirations, gender stereotyping in jobs and in society as a whole, lack of access to education and specialized training, entry-level barriers, discriminatory promotion practices and the double burden of family and career responsibilities and obsolete perceptions of them, which affect even those who have no children.

These negative factors were also identified in the case-studies. Particular attention was paid to the first and the last. In Venezuela, women's managerial capacities were said to be underrated, and men were suspicious and mistrustful of female superiors. Hostile attitudes of male co-workers was cited as a factor which held

---

[41] Cited in J. Bayes, 'Women in public administration: A speculative typology', paper presented at the International Political Science Association Roundtable for Sex Roles and Politics Research Committee, Hunter College, New York City, 1-2 June 1990.

women back in India. In Costa Rica, there was said to be discrimination against women who tried to involve themselves in areas traditionally held to be male. Conservative social attitudes and misconceptions about 'feminine nature' kept Algerian women out of responsible posts. In the United Republic of Tanzania, women in the civil service had to prove themselves and have more experience than their male counterparts in order to be accepted.

The case-studies suggest that even in the public sector, the workplace is not an environment where women can balance their family and employment responsibilities. The Tanzanian women had to cope with almost no job-related support facilities. Trade unions in India regarded wage disparities between women and men and the lack of maternity benefits and crèches as unimportant. The dearth of child-care facilities and the uncompromising approach of rigid personnel officers militated against women's professional progress in the Netherlands.

Moreover, promotion practices that discriminated against women were illustrated in the Greek study. When promotion was an automatic process based on seniority, women benefited, but when there was strong competition for vacancies, women tended to lose out to men. The absence of women on the committees responsible for promotion was held to be significant.

In response to the low proportion of women in management and decision-making in public administration, many countries have adopted policies designed to assist women to rise to the upper levels of the civil service, to counter discrimination, to create equal opportunities for men and women and to strengthen women's status in the workforce. In the United States, for example, women, ethnic minorities and disabled people have been the target of specific affirmative action programmes in order to encourage their participation in the workforce generally and in the civil service especially. In Austria, the Programme for the Promotion of Women was established with the dual objectives of advancing equal opportunities for women in the civil service and setting an example to the private sector of the economy. It sought to do this through non-discriminatory hiring practices, education and training programmes for women and the development of specific programmes in every department. India also made special efforts to attract women into the civil service through media campaigns and training incentives. New regulations about the posting of married couples, the mandatory presence of at least one woman on recruitment boards and the establishment of separate registers of women to ensure that they made up, if possible, at least 30 per cent of every list of prospective candidates, also aimed to enhance the prospects of women in the public sector.

The overall conclusion is that despite the great cultural, ideological and economic differences between countries, women in public administration around the world appear to face similar problems. Better education and training have given increasing numbers of women access to civil service jobs and Governments are now major employers of female labour. Yet in spite of the influx of women over the last decade, there has been no proportional increase in their presence in top-level positions. Most countries have some women in senior administrative positions, but they are few.

CHAPTER IV
EQUALITY IN POLITICAL DECISION-MAKING: AN EMPIRICAL VIEW

The formal institutional power to formulate the policies upon which the well-being of all citizens depends is vested variously in a country's legislature, its government executive and the higher echelons of the civil service. Regardless of the systems of which they are a part, these institutions can play a crucial role in the empowerment of a nation's women. Yet, as the previous chapters show, very few women share in this power or participate in making the decisions that affect their lives. Although most women have the de jure right to be part of these processes, in practice they continue to be underrepresented at every level, and many barriers still stand between them and the equality with men to which they are entitled. It should be recalled that there was not a single woman in the legislature of 11 of the 124 countries for which data was available in 1989, and the average representation was only 9.7 per cent. With a proportion of only 4.2 per cent, the situation was even worse in the upper levels of national Governments in 1987. Data from 153 countries revealed that in 60 per cent of them there were no women at all in the ministerial ranks.

An examination of the characteristics of those countries where women have an above-average level of participation suggests several groups of possible factors that might be related to better access. These include the country's level of economic development, since many of the countries with above-average levels of women in decision-making are wealthier. Female educational levels and labour force participation rates are also important. Internal practices and attitudes that determine training and promotion in public organizations and gender ideology can have a marked effect.

Many of the identified barriers to women's advancement, including the structure and method of operation of national bureaucracies, or the extent to which women are supported in their efforts to reconcile work and domestic responsibilities (whether by public services or by sharing of these responsibilities between women and men) are not yet susceptible to quantitative analysis. Enough comparable statistics on the status of women now exist at the national level and in United Nations statistical series to permit an examination of some of the factors associated with higher or lower levels of women's participation in decision-making. This chapter relates United Nations demographic, political and economic statistics relevant to the status of women to women's participation in parliament and high-level decision-making in the 155 countries covered in the study.

WOMEN IN PARLIAMENT AND IN GOVERNMENT DECISION-MAKING

The presence of women in parliament and in high positions in Governments and administrations has thus far been considered separately. This is to highlight the fact that the processes involved in selection are often different. It is important to see whether there is a relationship between the two. The question is the extent to which changing the composition of the parliament, which can be done by the vote, is likely to change the composition of government decision-making. As has been noted, women can reach government decision-making by a number of paths, including the formal civil service. To what extent a larger proportion of women in parliament makes these paths easier is the policy question to be considered by women in terms of voting.

To examine this question, a correlation was made between the proportion of women in national parliaments and women in high-level government jobs. The correlation compared data for 1987. The absence of information on changes over time in women in decision-making (because as of 31 May 1991 only one study, covering 1987, has been made on the issue) makes it difficult to propose a causal relationship between the two variables. It would be expected that a positive correlation between women in parliament and in government decision-making is likely, because in many countries the members of the executive are chosen from the legislature and so the more women in parliament, the larger the pool of potential women ministers and vice-ministers.

The percentage of female parliamentarians is usually considerably higher than the representation of women in cabinet or high level government positions (see figure VIII). This holds true even taking the recent changes in the composition of parliaments in Eastern Europe at the end of the 1980s into account.

Figure VIII. Percentage of women in parliament and government decision-making, 1987

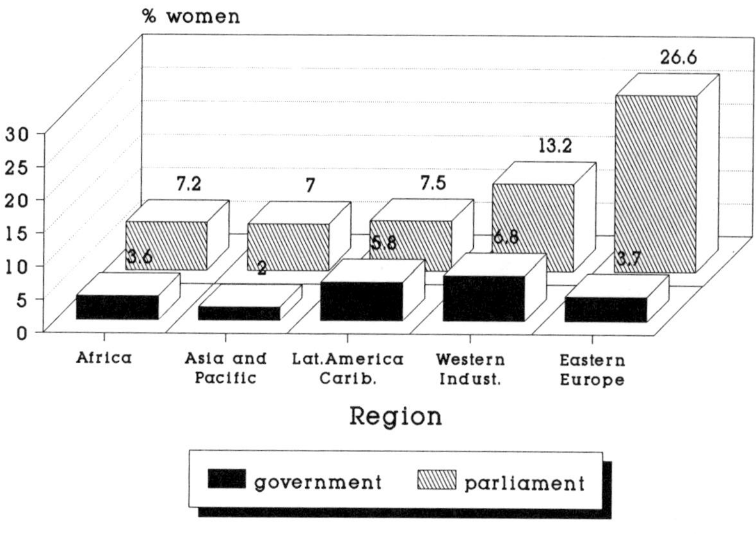

The overall correlation between the percentage of women in parliament and the presence of women in the top four levels of government decision-making is 0.34. (See figure IX on the interpretation of correlation coefficients.) The correlation is even higher between women in parliament and in ministerial level positions. For that it is 0.45. This means that, in general, the more women in parliament, the more in government decision-making, especially at the ministerial level.

Figure IX. The Pearson correlation

The Pearson correlation compares values for the same countries on two variables. In the first case, the variables are percentages of women in parliament and percentages of women in government decision-making. If there was a perfect positive match by country between scores on both variables the correlation would have a value of 1.0. This would mean that the country with the highest value on percentage of women in parliament was also the one with the highest on women in government, the second highest on one was the second highest on the other and so forth down to the lowest value on women in parliament that had the lowest score on women in government. If there was a perfect negative match by country, the correlation would be –1.0. This would mean that the country with the highest value on women in parliament had the lowest value on women in government decision-making and so on through the country with the lowest value on women in parliament having the highest value on women in government. If there was no relationship between the two variables, meaning that the scores did not match at all, the correlation would be 0.0.

In practice, most correlations include cases that deviate from perfection, because they summarize a variety of other factors and arrangements. Some of the deviations can occur by change. For that reason, correlation statistics usually are tested to see the probability that they could have occurred by chance.

This tends to support the conclusion that the parliament is a major source of recruitment of ministers. It also supports the conclusion that the general political advancement of women (reflected in the percentage of women among those elected to parliament) carries over to government decision-making. However, the conclusion differs by region. Women's representation in both political and administrative decision-making is highest in the Western industrialized countries followed by countries in the Latin-American and Caribbean region (see figure VIII). It is lowest in the region of Asia and the Pacific. However, in all regions the average percentage of women in decision-making is lower than in parliament.

The correlation between the proportion of women in parliament and in decision-making is generally positive in all regions, as can be seen in figure X. However, the patterns vary considerably by region and the exceptions are instructive. In Western industrialized countries, the correlation is strongest between women in parliament and women at the ministerial and vice-ministerial levels of decision-making. Most of the countries involved have parliamentary systems, in which the ministers and vice-ministers are usually drawn from the parliament. However, at the senior levels of the civil service, there is even a negative correlation between women in parliament and in decision-making. This reflects the fact that improvement in the representation of women in the political sphere has not yet affected the civil service.

Figure X. Correlations between women in parliament and in government decision-making, 1987

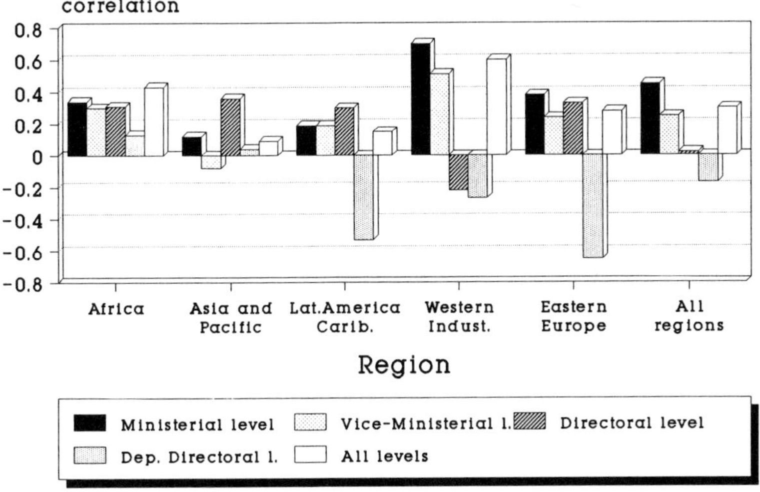

The gap between the high percentages in the legislature in Eastern Europe in 1987 and the low percentages in the ranks of the decision makers suggests that reserving a specific number of seats for women in the former does not influence the rate of their recruitment to high government positions. In this region, as in other places, it is possible to hypothesize that the higher proportion of women in the parliaments reflected the relatively weaker role of these bodies. The more powerful the institution, the less women to be found prominent in it. However, the same pattern appears in Latin America and the Caribbean and it is not clear that in the countries of that region, the parliaments are less powerful.

While the presence of women in parliament is no guarantee that women will be found in other areas of decision-making, it is clear that where women are absent from parliament, it is unlikely that they will be found in other jobs. In 9 of the 11 countries in which there were no women in parliament in 1987, there were no women in important executive or administrative positions either. The countries included Antigua and Barbuda, Comoros, Djibouti, Jordan, Lebanon, Morocco, Solomon Islands, United Arab Emirates and Yemen. Although there were no female parliamentarians in Uruguay or Papua New Guinea, 7.1 and 4.9 per cent, respectively, of their high officials were women.

Economic and social factors related to participation in decision-making

The regional differences in participation suggest that levels of economic and social development affect women's chances to participate in politics and decision-making. If so, it could be argued that women's political participation is contingent upon achieving a certain level of development. Indeed, some of the development theories of earlier decades have suggested this. In order to investigate this question further a number of indicators were analysed.

Two economic and one demographic indicators were used: per capita gross domestic product (GDP), annual rate of population growth and the percentage of government expenditure devoted to the public sector. Per capita GDP is a standard indicator of the wealth of a country. Development is measured in terms of it: countries above a certain level are considered developed, those below it are considered developing.[42] However, only the value of what is produced in the formal economy is reflected in this figure and it does not necessarily mean that the society is able to meet the material or non-material needs of all its members.

The analysis used the figures for 1985, given in United States dollars. For the 77 countries for which data are available for both per capita GDP and for women in decision-making, there is no correlation. That is, no pattern emerged that suggested that wealthy countries had more women in parliament or in decision-making posts. Looking at individual regions did not change the result. In some, there were more women in decision-making at lower levels of per capita GDP than at higher; in others the reverse was true. Within the regions, there was considerable variation in levels of per capita GDP. The meaning of these differences, however, is that wealth, even relative wealth among developing countries, is not a prerequisite for women in decision-making.

There is a positive statistical correlation between a low (less than 1 per cent) rate of population growth and a relatively high proportion of women in parliament (an average of 17.1 per cent) and official decision-making (5.8 per cent). The average representation in countries where the growth rate was more than 3 per cent was 6

---

[42] In 1987, none of the countries of Eastern Europe reported GDP figures, because they used a different system of national accounts. They are accordingly not included in this analysis.

per cent in parliament and 2.6 per cent in high government posts. This correlation is apparent in all regions except Eastern Europe where again macro-level factors did not appear to affect women's participation in the legislature.

The hypothesis that higher public expenditure and greater government employment might mean more opportunity for women was confirmed in the 72 countries for which data were available: the more money allocated to the public sector, the more women in high-level positions. The correlation coefficient was 0.32 between the percentage of government expenditure of GDP and the percentage of women among parliamentarians. The coefficient for government decision-making was 0.28. There was no correlation with ministerial decision-making levels. The case was particularly marked in Africa and the Western industrialized countries. Because GDP figures were not produced in Eastern Europe in 1987, that region was not included in the analysis.

The relationship between public expenditure and women in decision-making is probably due to the fact that more resources are spent for public goods, of which education is one of the most important. The availability of educational opportunity for women, both as a precondition for individual professional advancement and to develop an electorate that can act autonomously is important. As the case-studies emphasize, almost all the women who have reached the top positions have had a higher education. Access to education and training stands out as a necessary condition for a career in politics and for gender-balanced political representation.

The educational opportunities easily available to women vary between countries and between regions. In Africa and Asia and the Pacific, for example, around three quarters of all women aged 25 years and over are illiterate, a rate much higher than for men.[43] Illiteracy is largely a reflection of educational opportunity. In Latin America and the Caribbean, Eastern Europe and Western industrialized countries, there are almost no differences on the basis of gender in terms of present-day school enrolment, but former inequalities still affect adult women. The state of educational opportunity, past and present, is an important factor in women's political participation.

The ratios of women to men in enrolment in different levels of education in 1970 and 1980 are indicators of the extent of equal educational opportunities. A ratio of 1.0 means that as many women as men were enrolled. A ratio lower than 1.0 would mean that women had less relative access to education. The indicator for 1970 is more telling, since children who were in the educational system in 1970 would be adults in the mid-1980s, when the statistics on women in parliament and in government decision-making were collected. It also implies something about educational access in earlier times, since changes in enrolment patterns are typically not rapid, but rather reflect underlying expansion of the educational system and increased attention to equality.

There is a moderate correlation between the ratio of girls to boys in primary

---

[43] 'The World's Women 1970-1990', p. 46.

education in 1970 and the percentage of women in parliament (0.30) and in government decision-making (0.23) in 1987. The correlations are slightly stronger between the ratio of girls to boys in secondary schools in 1970 and women in parliament (0.35) and government decision-making (0.27) in 1987. There was no correlation between these indicators and the percentage of women at ministerial levels.

The importance of an educated electorate, and a pool from which women can be drawn for the civil service, seems to be confirmed by these findings. There is also some hope that as educational equality, which continues to improve in all regions, has its long-term effect, the prospects for women's political participation will improve.

Since most women political leaders are recruited from the educated and professional groups, the ratio of women to men in enrolment in third-level education in 1970 is an indicator of the extent to which women had equal access to university education. As can be seen from tables 14 and 15, there is a generally positive relationship between third-level education access and decision-making: the higher the proportion of girls in tertiary education in 1970, the higher the proportion of women in decision-making in parliament and government in 1987.

Table 14. Percentage of women in parliament in 1987 and ratio of women to men in university-level education in 1970

Region	Ratio of women to men in third-level education				
	Less than .20	.20-.29	.30-.49	.50-.79	80 or more
Africa	6.6	6.7	2.7	16.0	24.0
Asia and the Pacific	4.6	10.4	3.0	7.5	8.3
Latin America and the Caribbean	-	7.0	7.5	12.1	4.4
Eastern Europe	-	-	28.8	28.3	25.2
Western industrialized countries	-	8.5	14.0	13.7	31.5
	-----	----	-----	-----	-----
All countries	6.3	8.4	9.7	14.5	17.0

Table 15. Percentage of women in government decision—making in 1987 and ratio of women to men in university-level education in 1970

Region	Ratio of women to men in third-level education				
	Less than .20	.20-.29	.30-.49	.50-.79	80 or more
Africa	4.5	5.4	2.1	1.4	14.6
Asia and the Pacific	0.7	1.0	0.5	3.7	5.3
Latin America and the Caribbean	-	9.7	1.9	4.7	8.9
Eastern Europe	-	-	4.5	5.9	2.1
Western industrialized countries	-	1.4	7.7	4.9	19.4
	-----	----	-----	-----	-----
All countries	4.0	4.1	4.2	4.5	7.6

While the general rule holds, there are a few exceptions. Sometimes that is because there are only a few countries in the category. In other cases, such as Eastern Europe, the existence of quotas for women in parliament in all countries means that differences in educational access would not influence parliamentary representation. The effect is clearly greater on parliaments, since the education-ratio is more indicative of the characteristics of the electorate than of the civil service.

In Africa, for example, one exception to the general finding was the category of .30-.49, which consisted of Egypt and Madagascar where the proportion of women in decision-making was lower than for countries with a less favourable ratio. Consistent with the general trend is the Seychelles, at one extreme in Africa, where the ratio between girls and boys in school in 1970 was above .80, and 24 per cent of its parliamentarians were women. Similarly, in Finland, where the ratio is at equality, 19.4 per cent of senior officials and 31.5 per cent of parliamentarians in 1987 were women.[44]

The extent to which women will be able to participate in politics may also be affected by their role in the labour market especially in the professional, technical,

[44] At its election in 1991, Finland increased the percentage of women parliamentarians to 38.4 per cent.

administrative and managerial occupations, from which public servants are recruited. To examine this, three groups of indicators were used, measuring women in the paid labour force and the types of occupation in which women were engaged.

An indicator of the extent to which women are found in the formal economy of a country is the percentage of women in the economically active population. This can be supplemented by the ratio of women to men in that population. Figures for 1980 show a clear correlation between women in paid work and women in decision-making: the higher their employment rate, the higher their participation in government. These figures are shown in tables 16 and 17.

Table 16. Percentage of women in parliament in 1987 and percentage of women in the economically active population in 1980

Region	Percentage of women in the economically active population				
	Less than 10	10-19	20-29	30-49	50 or more
Africa	5.8	5.3	7.3	4.2	16.0
Asia and the Pacific	4.4	8.0	-	7.7	7.2
Latin America and the Caribbean	-	1.6	6.3	9.2	7.7
Eastern Europe	-	-	52.5	16.5	36.1
Western industrialized countries	-	3.0	6.4	11.3	21.3
All countries	5.0	5.5	4.2	4.5	19.6

Table 17. Percentage of women in government decision-making in 1987 and of women in the economically active population in 1980

Region	Percentage of women in the economically active population				
	Less than 10	10-19	20-29	30-49	50 or more
Africa	3.7	3.8	7.2	1.6	0.0
Asia and the Pacific	0.5	1.3	2.1	2.4	5.7
Latin America and the Caribbean	-	0.0	4.6	4.4	9.8
Eastern Europe	-	-	13.9	3.2	2.0
Western industrialized countries	-	0.0	0.0	6.3	11.5
	-----	----	-----	-----	-----
All countries	2.0	5.5	4.9	4.5	7.2

Female employment was high in a number of countries from Eastern Europe and from the group of Western industrialized countries. Where more than half the women were in paid work, the proportion of female parliamentarians was almost 20 per cent, a figure well above the overall world average of 9.7 per cent. This pattern was generally found in every region.

Using a slightly different indicator — the ratio of women to men in the economically active population — the same result is found. There is a correlation of 0.34 between a higher ratio and a higher percentage of women in parliament. Women are more likely to be in parliament in those countries where women are also in the workplace.

The same positive correlation can be observed between women in employment and women in decision-making: where women make up a greater proportion of the workforce, more women are involved in governmental decision-making. However, although this association is clear in Asia and the Pacific, Latin America and the Caribbean and the Western industrialized countries, it is more difficult to interpret the figures in Africa, where the percentage of women considered to be in the economically active population is under 20 per cent in most countries, and only rises above this in four countries.

The contrary can be observed in the Eastern European countries, in most of which a majority of adult women were employed and therefore made up half or more of the labour force. In those countries, as already noted, women are not found in large numbers in governmental decision-making levels.

In terms of the indicator of equality, the ratio of women to men in the economically active population, there is also a positive correlation (0.24) with the percentage of women in government decision-making, but it is less strong than for women in parliament.

The kind of employment that women typically have is also important. Two types of occupation are particularly important in this context: professional or technical occupations and administrative and managerial occupations. Both categories are heterodox. Unfortunately, data on type of occupation were only available for slightly over half the countries. For these countries, there is a correlation between type of occupation and incidence of women in decision-making: the more women in professional employment, the more women to be found in governmental decision-making. The correlation between the ratio of women to men in professional and technical occupations and the percentage of women in governmental decision-making was fairly strong at 0.30. The correlation was even stronger with the ratio of women to men in administrative and managerial occupations (0.39).

This suggests that advancement of women into governmental decision-making positions is enhanced when there are more potential recruits in professional, administrative and managerial occupations. There is a complete lack of correlation between these occupational variables and the proportion of women in parliament, further suggesting that the effect is in terms of recruitment.

POLITICAL STRUCTURAL FACTORS

At the international intergovernmental level, no agreed method of classifying countries according to political structure yet exists. The exercise would be a difficult one in any case, given the differences between them. Nevertheless, as has been suggested, the type of political system may affect the likelihood of women reaching decision-making levels. Two variables were explored in this context: the length of time women had had the right to vote and the number of legal political parties existing in the country in 1987.

It would be plausible to assume that the more experience women had in voting, the more they would vote in their interest and elect other women to parliament and create a climate in which women would reach decision-making posts. As noted in chapter I, above, in many countries there was a very long gap between the time women received the legal right to vote and hold office and the time when they were actually elected to parliaments or entered cabinets. In fact, there is a strong correlation (0.43) between the number of years that women in a country have had the right to vote and the percentage of women in parliament. There is also a strong correlation with the percentage of women at ministerial levels (0.38). The implication is that women eventually begin to use their rights to affect the composition of parliaments and, through them, government.

The highest proportions of women in parliament are found in those places where women had the right to vote before 1940, where the average in 1987 was 16.7 per cent. It fell to 12.1 per cent in countries where women's suffrage was granted between 1940 and 1950, to 5.8 per cent when it was adopted between 1950 and 1960 and 6 per cent where they were first allowed to vote between 1960 and 1970. However, it is interesting to note that the average was 8.8 per cent in countries where universal suffrage has been established since 1970, most simultaneously with independence. In this particular case, there are no major differences by region.

The number of political parties is another structural variable. It can be asked whether women are more likely to be involved in decision-making if there is a party competition. A comparison of countries according to the number of political parties shows that the average percentage of women elected to parliament in 1987 in 44 countries with a single political party or no parties at all is higher (11.1 per cent) than for the 75 countries with a multi-party system (9.1 per cent).[45] This result is generally consistent across regions, although the incidence of one-party systems is infrequent in some regions. For example, of the countries of Latin America and the Caribbean, only Cuba had a one-party State (and a high percentage (33.9) of women in parliament). Among the Western industrialized countries there was none with a single- or no-party system. The relatively higher percentage of women in parliament in single-party systems, may reflect the practice of reserving seats for various groups, including women, in some of them. It may also reflect the point made previously, that in some systems, particularly those in which there is no inter-party competition, the parliaments may have a less decisive role.

This latter conclusion is supported by the data in table 18, which shows the average percentage of women in government decision-making in terms of whether the countries have single- or multi-party systems. As can be seen, the percentages are uniformly higher in countries with multi-party systems in 1987, except for the few in Eastern Europe that formally had a multi-party system, albeit with a dominant major party.

---

[45] Derbyshire and Derbyshire, op. cit.

Table 18. Average percentage of women in government decision-making by number of political parties, 1987

Region	One or no party	Two or more political parties
Africa	3.3	4.5
Asia and the Pacific	1.4	2.7
Latin America and the Caribbean	2.7	6.3
Eastern Europe	4.4	2.3
Western industrialized countries	-	6.8
	-----	----
All countries	2.8	5.3

While it would be difficult to generalize from these cases, the relatively impressive record of the Nordic countries, already noted in chapter II above, in bringing women into decision-making, suggests that structural factors combine. All of those countries have a long tradition of democracy, political competition, concern for women's legal rights, as well as systems that emphasize compromise rather than conflict in the political process.

General status of women

A fundamental issue is the general relationship between the level of equality between women and men, and access to political power and high-level decision-making. Is the advancement of women a precondition for equality in political participation and decision-making, or is equality in political participation a precondition for the further advancement of women? The question cannot be answered empirically at this time since there are few time-based statistics on which a model could be built, but it is possible to test whether there is a relationship between equality in non-political areas and equality in politics.

There is no generally accepted composite indicator of women's advancement, although there are moves towards developing such indicators within the United

Nations system.[46] However, one composite indicator was developed by the Population Crisis Committee, a private non-governmental organization based in the United States. This was used in the present analysis to provide a general overview of the status of women.[47] The index, based on official statistics, seeks to measure women's well-being according to national figures relating to health, marriage and children, education, employment and social equality. In each area, three indicators are used. For example, in terms of education, indicators include the percentage of women who are secondary school teachers, female primary and secondary school enrolment ratios and the female university enrolment ratio. Countries were generally classified in terms of their scores on these sub-indices in terms of high, medium or low.

There was a clear relationship between the various indicators of women's status and the percentage of women in parliament and in government decision-making. In effect, the average percentage was 1.3 per cent for countries with low equality in employment, 2.8 per cent for countries that scored in the middle range and 6.0 per cent for countries with high scores. The findings were similar for other sub-indices. They were also similar in terms of the percentage of women in parliament.

The relationship of the composite indicator of women's status with women in decision-making is clear: the higher the score on women's general status, the higher the percentage of women in parliament and in government decision-making. This relationship is shown in table 19. The patterns are consistent across regions, although the regions themselves differ in terms of the proportion of countries having different scores on the index, as can be seen in figure XI.

Table 19. Average percentage of women in decision-making in countries grouped by score on the composite index of status of women, 1987

Score on composite index of women's status	Percentage of women in government decision-making	Percentage of women in parliament
Low	1.5	4.4
Low middle	3.7	6.0
High middle	4.6	8.6
High	6.8	20.4

[46] United Nations Development Programme, Human Development Report, 1991 (New York, Oxford University Press, 1991); see also The Worlds Women 1970-1990.

[47] Population Crisis Committee, 'Poor, Powerless and Pregnant: Country rankings on the Status of Women' (Washington, D.C, 1988).

Figure XI. Percentage of women in government decision-making in terms of scores on a composite women's status measurement, 1987

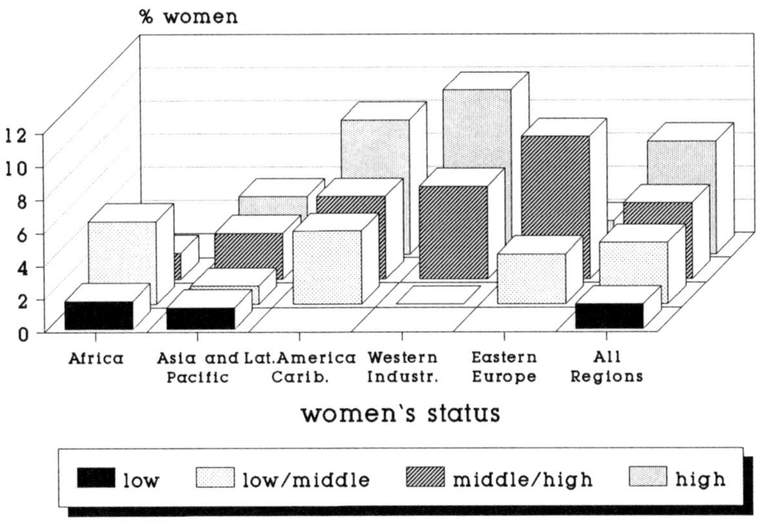

While there are no internationally-accepted composite indicators of the status of women, adherence to the Convention on the Elimination of All Forms of Discrimination against Women reflects a country's desire for gender equality and a broad indication of its acceptance of international norms relating to the status of women. The Convention came into force in September 1981, and by 1 September 1991 it had been ratified or acceded to by 108 countries, rich and poor, developed and developing, from every region. In spite of their economic diversity, these countries share a strong commitment to equality between the sexes. Another 10 countries had signed the Convention by that date.

For most countries, ratification or acceding to the Convention means that national laws have been made or are being made consistent with the international standards set out in the Convention. Signature means acceptance of the principles and an intention to ratify once national legislation has been appropriately adjusted. Those countries that have not ratified have different reasons, but clearly they lack the same level of commitment to equality as those countries that have ratified, acceded to or signed the Convention.

A country that ratifies or accedes to the Convention can enter reservations on those articles which, for various reasons, are incompatible with national laws. Many of these are procedural in nature (e.g. inability to accept the jurisdiction of the International Court of Justice in arbitration of disputes). Some, however, include reservations based on custom, religion or tradition to articles concerning women's role in society.

Countries can be classified according to whether they have ratified or acceded to the Convention with substantive reservations, have ratified with substantive reservations, have signed but not ratified or have neither signed nor ratified. Analysis according to these categories has previously been made to assess the relationship between the status of the Convention and statistical indicators of women's status as part of a larger examination of the relationship between international norms and the practice of religion.[48]

Consistent with the other indicators of the status of women, it is obvious that countries that have ratified or acceded to the Convention without reservation and those that have signed without ratifying have higher average percentages of women in decision-making, whether in government or in parliaments (see table 20).

Table 20. Average percentage of women in government and in parliament, by status of the Convention on the Elimination of All Forms of Discrimination against Women, 1987

Classification	Number of countries	Percentage of women in government decision-making	Percentage of women in parliament
Ratified, no reservations	90	5.6	8.4
Ratified with substantive reservations	12	2.3	5.8
Signed only	12	5.1	8.8
Neither signed nor ratified	42	2.4	6.0

[48] Valentine M. Moghadem, ed., 'Identity Politics and Women: Cultural Reassertions and Feminism in International Perpective' (forthcoming in the World Institute for Development Economics Research (WIDER) of United Nations University series in development published by Clarendon Press).

The extent that substantive reservations on key articles of the Convention reflect a lack of acceptance of the principles of women's full equality would explain the finding in table 20 that countries cluster between unreserved ratifiers and signatories, and countries that have either ratified with substantive reservations or not accepted the Convention at all.

The pattern is similar at the regional level, as can be seen from figure XII, with a few exceptions. The most dramatic is in Latin America and the Caribbean. This was caused by several Caribbean countries that had not become parties to the Convention at the time of the analysis (1987), but who, like other Caribbean countries, had a relatively high percentage of women in government decision-making. All these countries - Belize, Bolivia, Grenada and Trinidad and Tobago - have since acceded to the Convention.

Figure XII. Percentage of women in government decision-making by status of the Convention on the Elimination of All Forms of Discrimination against Women, 1987

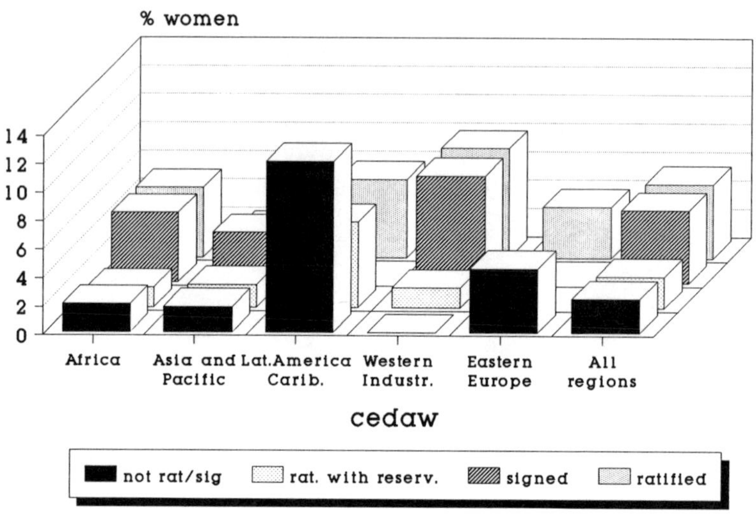

The clear correlation between gender equality and women in high-level decision-making does not answer the question of which comes first. However, there is no question that during the past 20 years the improved general status of women in society ultimately led to an increase in women's participation in decision-making. However this has not happened everywhere, and in most countries the level of women's participation in decision-making is not very high.

The fact that change in women's participation in decision-making in some countries has been relatively rapid suggests that this aspect of the advancement of women can precede others, but there is virtually no information available to test this assumption.

WHAT DIFFERENCE WOULD MORE PARTICIPATION MAKE?

The issue of what would be implied by increased participation of women in politics and decision-making must be left unresolved, at least in terms of aggregate statistical analysis. It can be reasonably assumed that the commitment of societies to women's social, economic, legal and cultural conditions would be increased if there were more women involved in political decision-making. It is important to examine the assumption that an augmented female presence in high places would alter the outcome of political deliberations, a concept that, together with the argument of democracy, is at the heart of the demand for more women in decision-making.

Surveys and research in a number of countries suggest that men and women differ in their opinions and attitudes towards public issues. It is reasonable to conclude that these gender differences will persist among politicians whose input into decision-making and public affairs will vary accordingly. Nor are the differing values and perspectives confined to the obvious sphere of women's rights. They extend to questions of peace and war, where women are frequently prominent in the support of peace, and of environmental and social service issues. Women are likely to have different domestic priorities that can alter political agendas significantly.

It can not be shown that the few women who have achieved political power have made a difference in a gender sense. It is usually argued that they have been too few in number and operating in a male domain. The argument continues that, in order to function effectively at decision-making levels on an equal footing, the female minority has had to adopt the male values that dominate the political culture and system. Research has suggested that only when a minority increases to about 30-35 per cent does it become strong enough to influence the fundamental group culture and form the alliances that can give it a significant impact on the whole. This argument indicates that the effect of women on the ambience and outcome of high-level decision-making will only be felt when their representation exceeds 35 per cent.

This 'critical mass' has only been achieved in a handful of countries, and so most research findings are based on the expressed attitudes of politicians and their perceptions of gender differences in approach and political behaviour. However, data have been analysed on the number and content of motions tabled by women parliamentarians. As their numbers have increased to the crucial point in some parliaments gender differences in terms of their impact and capacity for change can be studied. For example, a study of elected officials in the United States showed considerable differences in male and female attitudes towards the economy, war and peace, nuclear energy, capital punishment, abortion and the Equal Rights Amendment. A study of voting patterns in the House of Representatives in that country covering the period from 1972 to 1980 supported these findings and indicated that regardless of their party affiliation or electoral district, women members tended to vote in what were considered more liberal ways than their male colleagues.[49]

Although politics in the Scandinavian countries were still dominated by men, there

---

[49] Centre for American Woman and Politics, 'Women Make a Difference' (Rutgers, New Jersey, Eagleton Institute of Politics, 1983) and S. Welch, 'Are women more liberal than men in the US Congress?', Legislative Studies Quarterly, volume X, No.1 (1985), pp. 125-134.

were major increases in women's participation in the late 1970s and 1980s. Consequently, more research on the question of the differences made by these increases has taken place in that region. One study of a suburban area near Stockholm where women's participation in local government rose to between 40 and 48 per cent in the 1980s found that the criteria for decision-making had broadened to include women's perspectives.[50] There was more emphasis on issues such as child-care, schooling and the organization of leisure. The climate of debate had been modified so that discussions became both more to the point and less harsh. The women used simpler, more concrete language which made the political debates more accessible to the general public. Male representatives felt able to acknowledge their family obligations and men even dared to admit that they could take priority over political concerns.

In Finland, women parliamentarians were found to have concerned themselves with bills related to social legislation and cultural and educational policies, while their male counterparts were more concerned with transport, public utilities and economic polity.[51] In Sweden, another study revealed that women's legislative proposals generally focused on education and social policies and that they rarely initiated legislation on financial items. Their male colleagues tended to concentrate on fiscal matters, trade and industry.[52] In the United Kingdom, a similar study analysed 25 bills introduced by female members of parliament and found a clear emphasis on concerns considered to be of interest to women: nine related to women and children, four to consumer issues and three each to alcohol or drunkenness and to the protection of animals.[53]

The issue requires further study as more experience is gained in those countries where women are beginning to form a larger proportion of parliaments and government decision-making, at different levels.

---

[50] S. Sinkonen, 'Women in local politics', in Unfinished Democracy: Women in Nordic Countries, E. Haavio-Manilla, ed. (Oxford, Pergamon Press, 1985).

[51] S. Sinkonen and E. Haavio-Manilla, 'The impact of the women's movement and legislative activity of women MPs on social development', in Women, Power and Political Systems, M. Rendel, ed. (London, Croon Helm, 1981), pp. 195-215.

[52] T. Skard and E. Haavio-Manilla, 'Women in parliament', Unfinished Democracy: Women in Nordic Countries,.pp. 54-80.

[53] Elizabeth Vallence, 1987., p. 90.

CHAPTER V
ACTION TO BE TAKEN

In the report of the Secretary-General entitled 'Equality: Equality in political participation and decision-making' (E/CN.6/1990/2, para. 5) it was stated that 'although the nature of politics differs in various national contexts and cultures and while women themselves are not in many respects a homogeneous group, one condition is common to all of them: they are not full participants in the public choices that affect their lives; and they are grossly underrepresented in politics and the civil service, especially at the decision-making levels'. It continued, 'The conditions have to be created in which there will be a sufficient number of women in decision-making positions, whether in politics or in the civil service, to make gender an unremarkable attribute and the selection of women for high positions inevitable and normal (E/CN.6/1990/2, para. 7)'.

The previous chapters have shown how much progress is required. With few exceptions, women are rarely found in the corridors of power. Only in the Nordic countries have conditions combined to place women at the centre of the political process in large enough numbers that the differences women make occur naturally such that, in that sense, gender has become an unremarkable attribute. Elsewhere in the world, the picture is largely uniform. There are differences, but they tend to be in terms of whether women are completely absent or merely present in small numbers. While there are indicators of improvement, recorded change is very slow. Whether the global target of equality can be achieved by the end of the next millennium, let alone by the end of the current century, is questionable. Yet, the fact that one group of countries could achieve the goal shows it is attainable. Examination of the factors involved, through comparison with global trends, can help to elucidate the steps which can be taken and can be expected to work. The analyses in the previous chapters suggest some of these.

EQUALITY IN POLITICAL PARTICIPATION

The previous chapters have included one of the first attempts to identify the economic, social and political factors statistically related to women's participation in decision-making. Taken together, they suggest the characteristics that would be found in countries if women were equal participants in public decision-making.

In the Nordic countries, the only group of countries where women are found in large numbers in decision-making, women have had the right to vote and stand for public office for many years, they have access to education and to employment. These countries have had steady rates of economic development, with much of the wealth earned redistributed through public programmes to achieve social equity. They have a tradition of democratic methods to determine national priorities, leadership and policies. And they have had a long-term commitment to gender equality. This combination suggests many of the characteristics that would be needed in a country for women to achieve equality in political participation and decision-making.

In such a model country, women would have the right to vote and stand for public office equal to that of men. In fact, women have that right in almost all countries in the world and have exercised it. This demonstrates that rights are a necessary condition for de facto equality but are not sufficient. In such a country women would have the same access as men to education and remunerated work. In many countries, however, even where the long-term effect of past discrimination means that women lack the same education as men and where their appearance in the formal labour force is recent, women have successfully entered politics in large numbers. Yet, in other countries, where equality in access to education and economic activity has been achieved, as in the Eastern European countries, women have not reached decision-making levels in real terms. While these conditions help, they are obviously not sufficient.

The ideal country would have a record of economic growth and incomes high enough that the average woman would not have to spend her entire day concerned about basic survival. There would be public resources to invest in programmes to foster social change and equality of opportunity. Yet among the wealthiest countries in the world, including those having the highest per capita national income of the countries classified as developing, are countries with the least equality in women's political participation. Alternatively, in many countries that are materially poor, women play a prominent place. Although material wealth is helpful, it is clearly not a determining factor.

Such a country would also have a long tradition of democratic political processes, in which women would have participated equally and as part of which they would have learned to express their interests peacefully through the ballot box and by holding public office. But in the average country, most adult women have had the opportunity of participating in the vote all of their lives, and this has been no guarantee that women will achieve decision-making positions. And there are countries in which, as part of a sudden change in government, women have emerged quickly in leadership roles. Obviously, tradition may help, but will not in itself lead to full equality.

In the ideal country there would be a recognition that democracy cannot be achieved without women's full participation in politics, as in other spheres of activity. There would be a commitment to equality, reflected in law and in national policy. And here the statistics are clear: the strongest correlation of a high percentage of women in decision-making is with indicators of that commitment to women's equality. Countries that have accepted international norms, embodied in the Convention on the Elimination of All Forms of Discrimination against Women, without reservation, do have a higher level of women in decision-making.

But if this commitment to democracy in fact as well as in theory is a necessary condition, is it a sufficient one?

WHICH COMES FIRST?

Correlations indicate the factors that combine, but not which come first. But which comes first is an essential question if strategies to achieve rapid change are sought. If progress of women into public decision-making positions is a result of general changes in the status of women, the focus should be on such underlying factors as education, employment and legal status. But the question is, to what extent is the general advancement of women needed before it is possible to have full participation in politics? Or, rather, is it the case that full participation in politics is necessary to achieve the general advancement of women?

In many respects, this is the issue of whether women are merely objects whose destinies are determined by the actions of others or the operation of anonymous forces of the market, or whether they are in control of their own destinies. Obviously if women are to be active in politics, they must be elected. For them to be elected, they must be put forward as candidates. However, in most countries, they are not. Thus, even if women wanted to use the political process to make changes by voting for women, at present they would not find any for whom to vote.

Women, as citizens, are most effective when informed. In that sense, the existence of an educated, informed electorate, as a consequence of women's equal access to education, is obviously helpful. And the ability of women to be economically independent, with comparable careers to men, can form the pool of qualified women from whom higher civil servants and political candidates can be drawn. But, the number of people who actually reach or compete for leadership positions is quite small. It would be hard to find any country where a large number of educated, economically independent women capable of competing for leadership positions could not be found. Therefore, the existence of a large population of educated, economically independent women is not a prerequisite.

Political power is subject to rapid change. Election results can change public policy and the distribution of power overnight. It is not necessary to wait for the impact of evolutionary processes. In theory, equality between women and men could be achieved in one parliamentary election, if half of the winners were women. In practice, the existence of established political institutions slows and orders the pace of change. But change can be forced. In Norway, for example, the transition from a polity in which women were a minority took only 20 years. It was the result of a consensus among women, but supported by men, that democracy was not possible without women's full participation and that women must share power. In 1969, only 9 per cent of members of parliament were women (which was the average for non-Nordic Western industrialized countries in 1987). By 1973, there were 16 per cent, and by 1985, the percentage had increased to 34.4.[54] Four parliamentary elections took place between 1969 and 1985.

This situation reflects a combination of factors: the fact that in many countries politics has been defined as a male domain; that women have not in the past held political positions; that women are perceived as not being able to win; that women as a group have voted the same as men and that there has been no advantage, politically, to promote women or women's issues among mainline politicians. These attitudes together constitute perhaps the fundamental immediate obstacle to women's full participation in politics and decision-making.

Selecting women as candidates

Obtaining more women candidates involves a number of steps in recruitment and selection. It means expanding the pool from which candidates can be recruited. It means inducing women in that pool to step forward and present themselves, taking the associated risks. And it means measures to ensure that they will be selected in fair numbers. Each has associated policy implications.

Expanding the pool

An argument sometimes used to justify the absence of women in high places is that there are insufficient numbers who are qualified. What constitutes qualification varies from country to country, but in most prior public activity and the existence of particular skills are essential. Ensuring that the pool of women who are considered qualified for recruitment is large, is a necessary step. On the one hand, it means giving women access to the career patterns that are considered acceptable for political leadership. On the other hand, it involves broadening the definition of experience that is considered desirable.

An essential step is for political parties, the source of much recruitment, to give women careers or experience within the parties similar to that of men. Active efforts should be made to recruit women into party leadership ranks. Responding to the complaint that there were not enough qualified women, the expert group meeting on decision-making suggested that information on potential women candidates should be compiled, maintained on a systematic basis and made available when candidacy or appointments were being considered.

Similarly, women's sections of parties should be evaluated and strengthened. Some argue that a women's section in a party, by becoming a form of a ghetto, hinders

---

[54] Norway, Royal Ministry of Foreign Affairs, 'Women in Norwegian Politics' (Oslo, 1989).

women in their progress. Others argue that such sections have accelerated the pace of progress. A consensus position is that a women's section needs to exist as long as women do not have full access to other aspects of the party. It should be a training ground for women political leaders and can serve the function of examining the women's dimension within the wider issues debated within the party. It will be prevented from becoming a ghetto to the extent that it makes input into policies and becomes a real source of recruitment.

The role of training within a party context was stressed. Training programmes should be developed to increase the political and management skills of women in politics, both as candidates and as elected or appointed officials, especially making use of the experience of other women who have achieved public office. The notion of mentoring, whereby experienced politicians identify and support newer recruits, has been emphasized. Similarly, training activities should be developed to make party members sensitive to the needs and potential of female members.

But expanding the pool also involves expanding the base from which candidates are chosen. In most societies, certain experiences and professions are considered political, while others are not so defined. That law is a profession from which politicians are often drawn is well-known, because of the training the profession gives in public speaking, negotiation and drafting of legislation. It is also a profession whose members allocate their time more flexibly than professions that must follow exact schedules. The types of profession into which women have typically been channelled have not been as highly considered as those typically occupied by men, nor have the experiences women are likely to have acquired in the community, usually of a voluntary and local type, been seen as relevant to higher level decision-making.

The expert group recommended that parties should be encouraged to examine the criteria used to select persons for political functions to ensure that the varieties of experience possessed by women are taken into account in selection.

Non-partisan organizations should consider developing their own programmes to develop women leaders, serving as yet another source of recruitment. Women's organizations were said to have a considerable potential role to play, especially in training women in political skill-building, media relations and resource generation.

Recognizing that much of political leadership is appointive rather than elective, and that experience in appointive office is considered valuable for the selection of candidates as well as for appointment to even higher office, means of increasing the appointment of women to advisory boards and similar positions were suggested.

Inducing women to put themselves forth

Seeking elective political office or appointive decision-making position involves taking risks. It means moving from a private sphere to a public one. It means being exposed to public criticism. The experience of women seeking public office, as has been noted, has not always been pleasant. Yet, when there are large enough numbers of women candidates, many of the negative effects of stereotypes disappear by themselves.

An essential step is the inculcation in women of the sense that without their participation, democracy cannot be achieved and more importantly, that they have the responsibility, as well as the right, to stand for public office. Efforts need to be undertaken actively to seek out potential women candidates and to train them in the type of skills necessary to succeed in obtaining public office. The mentoring mentioned above is one such means.

The transition from private to public spheres inevitably involves the mass media. These can reinforce old stereotypes or create new images. They can retard the incorporation of women into politics or promote it. There is no doubt that in many countries women politicians are treated differently in the media than are men. In some countries, the mass media are self-regulating, in others they are more directly subject to public control. The issue is how to ensure fair treatment of women by the media, by which is meant ensuring that women are not treated differently than male candidates either in terms of exposure or type of coverage. The expert group restricted itself to recommending that effective measures should be adopted to ensure the fairness of the media towards women in public life, including legislation if necessary. There is clearly a role for women's organizations in monitoring media performance.

It is often argued that women's double burden of work and domestic responsibilities make their participation difficult. There is no doubt that, on average, women today devote more time to domestic responsibilities than men and that this affects the way in which they allocate their time. This can be particularly important when women, particularly during child-bearing years, enter the lower rungs of the political ladder. Adjusting the scheduling of political activities to women's needs and providing support services such as child-care, and increasing the amount of sharing of responsibilities between spouses will all facilitate the recruitment of more women into the political process. At levels of top leadership, it is questionable whether the double burden is a major constraint. The levels are usually achieved for men and women when child-bearing and intensive child-rearing are largely completed and when economic reserves allow the necessary support to be obtained.

Ensuring that women are selected

Positions on party lists and tickets are inherently scarce political goods. In most democratic societies there are more potential candidates than places. Obtaining these slots is often considered a reward for past performance. The selectors themselves initially tend to be men, who themselves have worked their way up. The issue is how to ensure that, rather than continuing to select men for posts, they select women. It is the classic problem of affirmative action: how can the results of past discrimination be overcome quickly.

While in an ideal world, women should be selected in proportion to their numbers based on the general principles of democracy, reality is such that this does not happen automatically. The Expert Group Meeting recommended that, 'as an interim measure, substantial targets, such as quotas or similar forms of positive action to ensure women's candidacy for office and participation in political party posts, should be adopted (E/CN.6/1990/2, annex, para. 22)'.

In the Nordic countries, quotas specifying maxima and minima for each sex in decision-making posts have been set in many political parties. In other countries, parties and other organizations work on the basis of targets, relying on moral suasion to implement the targets. The main concern is that the targets should be used to provide for a breakthrough by women by being floors, below which women's representation is not allowed to fall. They should not become ceilings, above which it cannot rise. What has developed is a concept of 'parity target' based on the notion that both men and women have a right to be represented roughly in accordance with their numbers. This is different from what might be called a 'minority quota', whose purpose is to ensure for a minority group a minimum level of representation.

Underlying all of these policies, however, must be an implicit threat that if policies to ensure women's selection as candidates and leaders are not adopted, the women in the electorate will cast their votes elsewhere. Indeed, without that incentive, it is doubtful if any system based on targets will succeed. And, if the threat is believed by party leaders, the attractiveness of women candidates will be assured.

Electing women candidates

Selection of women as candidates is not a final step to ensuring women's participation in decision-making. First, women must be elected. As noted, the history of women as candidates is varied. There is some evidence that it has been easier for women to increase their proportion of candidates elected in systems with multi-member electoral constituencies rather than in single-member districts. This probably has more to do with the problems of defeating incumbents than to the system itself and, in any case, each political system is not easy to change. Rather, electing women to office has to do both with the candidates and with the electorate.

Equipping the electorate

Political research provides mixed evidence on when the electorate is more likely to support women candidates. Clearly, women have to have a sense that voting for candidates that support their interests is important. This implies that women's interests are clearly set out. It also implies convincing voters that those interests are likely to be furthered by supporting women candidates.

The role of women's organizations in raising this type of consciousness is important. As the Expert Group Meeting affirmed, 'Women's organizations should increase their participation in civic and political education, including the formation of groups to lobby actively for their interests (E/CN.6/1990/2, annex, para. 32)'.

There is also a need to seek media balance during an election campaign. Again, the existence of media monitoring by women's organizations can be helpful until media styles become gender-neutral.

In many political systems, the need to find substantial funding for campaigning is an obstacle for new candidates. When it is the party rather than the individual who runs, this is less of a problem. But individual campaigns inevitably favour the incumbents who, in most countries, are usually men. For this reason, a recommendation was made by the Expert Group Meeting that 'as an interim measure where the electoral system might make it useful, parties should undertake special measures to provide funding for women candidates for office (E/CN.6/1990/2, annex, para. 28)'.

Equipping the candidates

Women candidates need to be equipped as well. While it is assumed that natural skills and talents will prevail, in practice politics requires organization, finance, management and public-speaking skills. For this reason, for new candidates, training and special support can be valuable.

It is assumed that democratic elections will be fair. Reality may be different, particularly when the electoral process is likely to lead to a change in power holders. As with all candidates, it is important that women candidates and their supporters be vigilant about how the electoral system is used.

GETTING WOMEN INTO PUBLIC SERVICE

The issue for women in the public service is less whether women will enter the civil service than whether they can advance within it. In most countries, the majority of civil servants are women. This may be because pay in the public sector is inferior to the private, or because it is easier to enforce equality in entrance to the public service than in the private sector. Regardless of the reason, women are concentrated at the bottom ranks of the civil service.

Ironically, women's advancement should be easier in the civil service than outside because the operation of bureaucracies according to Weberian principles is expected to follow rational and therefore gender-neutral rules and procedures. The criteria for recruitment and career development in the public bureaucracy should not in theory discriminate against women. But their application obviously has worked against women in almost all countries. Indeed, the finding that there are relatively fewer women at the director level in government decision-making than at the ministerial level reflects the difficulty women have faced in advancing in the career civil service.

Fortunately, because civil services are open to scrutiny by the public the possibility exists for them to be studied and conclusions drawn, even though, in practice, few such studies have been made. The Expert Group Meeting made a number of suggestions on how barriers to women's advancement to senior ranks could be removed.

In order to ensure that women can not be discriminated against because of lack of information, all civil services should have clear statements on all personnel practices. This includes practices concerning recruitment and appointment, promotion, training and development, leave entitlements and other conditions of service, including appeal mechanisms.

Where possible, women should serve on all committees, especially appointment and promotion committees. In most public services, it is peer committees that serve as gatekeepers for admission to higher ranks. As long as these are exclusively in the hands of male civil servants, experience shows that, whether consciously or not, the boards will not be as sympathetic towards the promotion of women as they might be.

Civil services should accept it as legitimate that equal employment opportunity and affirmative action strategies are a necessary part of human resource management. In that sense, the disadvantages that women experience in their pursuit of career development vis-à-vis men should be mitigated.

An equitable distribution of women throughout all levels in the administrative hierarchy should be promoted to avoid concentrations at the lowest levels and in all functional areas (especially in areas regarded as non-traditional for women). How to do that should be a matter of national policy. Many countries have found it necessary to set targets or even more mandatory forms of affirmative action to ensure that women are adequately represented at the higher ranks of the civil service.

Unlike political election, the processes of change in public administrations are not usually rapid. The relatively smaller pools of women at higher ranks reflects earlier lack of opportunity for advancement. However, the large number of qualified women who had been earlier passed over can provide a pool for closing the gap quickly if appropriate policies are adopted.

Getting women into leadership

Once women are at decision-making levels, the question becomes one of avoiding the creation of a new sexual division of labour. Traditionally, women have been given responsibility for social areas but not economic or political ones. Other than tradition, there is no good reason for this, as the experience of the increasing number of women who have taken on leadership positions in non-traditional areas shows. Avoidance of putting women into 'leadership ghettos' is a function of the number of women in decision-making. If there are only a few, they will tend to be placed into traditional slots. If they are many, there is no alternative to many sharing power. The process is cumulative. Once women have occupied positions of power, these positions cease to be thought of as inherently masculine. Power in politics is based as much on the individual leader's constituency as on her personal merits. Leverage derives from independence, and independence derives from the political base.

Thus, in the end, the issue of women in politics and decision-making returns to the same point: if women wish to share power, and they should, they must put themselves forward as candidates for office, both elective and appointive, and they must be backed by other women, and men, who believe in this essential application of the principles of democracy. As the Expert Group Meeting states (E/CN.6/1990/2, annex, para. 1):

> Equality in political participation and decision-making is one of the major priorities for advancement of women into the 1990s. Without success in this area, other areas of advancement of women will be put at risk. Equity strategies directed at increasing the number of women in decision-making positions have to challenge, simultaneously, outdated ideas of women's place, worth and potential by improving the general position of women in society, and removing their generally lower social status and the low value placed on the work they perform.

ANNEX I
METHODOLOGICAL ISSUES

Regional groupings

The analysis primarily utilizes regional groupings of countries and areas in the same way as in The World's Women 1970-1990, which is on the basis of the practice of the Statistical Office of the United Nations. The groupings are found in annex III of that publication. There is one exception. The category of 'developed regions' used in that publication has been divided in this book into two subcategories to reflect differences in political and economic systems at the time of the data. One subcategory includes Eastern European countries (see table 4). The other category 'Western industrialized countries' includes all remaining countries in the Statistical Office' 'developed regions' category.

Sources of economic and social data

The statistical information on the basis of which much of the analysis was made in chapter IV is derived from the Women's Indicators and Statistics Data Base, a computerized database compiled by the United Nations Statistical Office. The information used in the current study is valid up to 1987, but most have been reported in the Compendium of Statistics and Indicators on the Situation of Women, 1986 (United Nations publication, Sales No. E/F.88.XVII.6).

Data on participation of women in parliament and in governmental decision-making

Indicators on women in parliament are based on data provided to the Inter-Parliamentary Union by national authorities and published periodically, most recently in 1988. Information on women's parliamentary representation in Eastern European countries was compiled from reports of the Union and from national reports to the United Nations.

Data on women in governmental decision-making are based on reports by individual Governments and published in the World-wide Government Directory, 1987-88. The indicators have been compiled from this source and analysed by the Division for the Advancement of Women, Centre for Social Development and Humanitarian Affairs of the United Nations Secretariat. Decision-making positions in Government were defined as ministers or equivalent, deputy or assistant ministers or equivalent, secretaries of state or permanent secretaries or equivalent, and deputy of state or director of Government or equivalent. Each country's entries in the Directory were classified according to the level and sector of the position and the sex of the occupant.

The category 'executive offices; economic, political and legal affairs' comprises the offices of the president or prime minister, and ministries such as finance, trade, industry and agriculture (economic); foreign affairs, interior and defence (political); and law and justice (legal). The category 'social affairs' comprises ministries such as health, education, housing and welfare.

ANNEX II
LIST OF DOCUMENTS

WORKING PAPERS

EGM/EPPDM/1989/WP.1 23 August 1989	Women and decision-making Prepared by the Division for the Advancement of Women, United Nations Office at Vienna
EGM/EPPDM/1989/WP.2 21 August 1989	Women in high-level political decision-making: A global analysis Prepared by Kathleen Staudt, Professor of Political Science, University of Texas, El Paso, United States of America
EGM/EPPDM/1989/WP.3 29 August 1989	The global and regional situation of women top civil servants Prepared by Denise K. Conroy, Lecturer in Public Administration, School of Management, Queensland University of Technology, Brisbane, Australia

CASE STUDIES

EGM/EPPDM/1989/CS.1 21 August 1989 egm/EPPDM/1989/CS.1/Corr.1 18 September 1989	Equality in political participation and decision making: the Philippine experience Prepared by the Honorable Santanina T. Rasul, Senator, Republic of the Philippines
EGM/EPPDM/1989/CS.2 23 août 1989	L'Espagne Etabli par Matilde Vázquez, Instituto de la Mujer, Ministerio de Asuntos Sociales, Madrid, Espagne
EGM/EPPDM/1989/CS.3 23 août 1989	L'Algerie Etabli par Leila Etteyeb, Alger, Algérie
EGM/EPPDM/1989/CS.4 29 August 1989	Poland Prepared by Renata Siemienska-Zochowska, Institute of Sociology, University of Warsaw, Poland
EGM/EPPDM/1989/CS.5 31 August 1989	Japan Prepared by Manae Kubota, Member of Parliament, Japan

EGM/EPPDM/1989/CS.6 1 September 1989	Greece Prepared by Eleni Stamiris, Mediterranean Women's Studies Institute, Athens, Greece
EGM/EPPDM/1989/CS.7 6 September 1989	Venezuela Prepared by Sonia Sgambatti, President, Inter-American Commission for Drug Abuse Control, Venezuela
EGM/EPPDM/1989/CS.8 13 September 1989	The Netherlands Prepared by Monique H. Leijenaar, Department of Political Science, University of Nijmegen, The Netherlands
EGM/EPPDM/1989/CS.9 14 September 1989	The participation of women in decision-making at the national level in Sweden Prepared by Karin Lindgren, Department of Peace and Conflict Research, Uppsala University, Sweden
EGM/EPPDM/1989/CS.10 18 September 1989	United Republic of Tanzania Prepared by the Honorable Gertrude I. Mongella, Minister without Portifolio, Member of Parliament, United Republic of Tanzania
EGM/EPPDM/1989/CS.11 18 September 1989	Costa Rica Prepared by Lena White Curling, Ombudsman for Women's Rights, Ministry of Justice, Costa Rica
EGM/EPPDM/1989/CS.12 19 September 1989	Equality in political participation and decision-making in Asia and the Pacific: The regional picture Prepared by Pari Soltan-Mohammadi, Regional Advisor on Women in Development, Economic and Social Commission for Asia and the Pacific, Bangkok, Thailand
EGM/EPPDM/1989/CS.13 19 September 1989	Women in public life Prepared by the Honorable Margaret Alva, Minister of State for Human Resource Development, Government of India
EGM/EPPDM/1989/CS.14 19 September 1989	Women and politics in Latin America and the Caribbean Prepared by the Women's Unit, Social Develop-

	ment Division, Economic Commission for Latin America and the Caribbean, Santiago, Chile
EGM/EPPDM/1989/CS.15 19 September 1989	United States of America Prepared by the Honorable Juliette C. McLennan, Representative of the United States of America to the Commission on the Status of Women
EGM/EPPDM/1989/CS.16 21 septembre 1989	Femmes-politque prise de décision Préparé par Pierette Biraud, Representante de la France à la Commission de la condition de la femme
EPPDM/1989/CS.17 21 September 1989	Union of Soviet Socialist Republics Prepared by Tatiana N. Nikolaeva, Representative of the Union of Soviet Socialist Republics to the Commission on the Status of Women
EGM/EPPDM/1989/CS.18 21 September 1989	Austria Prepared by Mechtild Petritsch-Holaday, Co-ordinator, International Women's Affairs, Federal Chancellery, Austria

INFORMATION PAPERS

EGM/EPPDM/1989/INF.1 10 July 1989	Information for participants
EGM/EPPDM/1989/INF.2/Rev.1 21 September 1989	List of participants
EGM/EPPDM/1989/INF.3/Rev.1 21 September 1989	List of documents
EGM/EPPDM/1989/INF.4/Rev.1 18 September 1989	Organization of work